Heaven Knows, Anything Goes

Dianne de la Vega

Order this book online at www.trafford.com/07-1378
or email orders@trafford.com

Most Trafford titles are also available at major online book retailers.

Illustrations: Carol DeMarinis
Cover Design & Photography: Todd Chandler

Certain names in this book have been changed
to protect the privacy of those individuals.

All Bible verses used are from the King James Version
unless otherwise noted.

130 Alta Avenue-D
Santa Monica, CA 90402
U.S.A.
www.diannedelavega.com

Note for Librarians: A cataloguing record for this book is available from Library
and Archives Canada at www.collectionscanada.ca/amicus/index-e.html

Printed in Victoria, BC, Canada.

ISBN: 978-1-4251-3540-9

PUBLISHING™

www.trafford.com

North America & international
toll-free: 1 888 232 4444 (USA & Canada)
phone: 250 383 6864 ♦ fax: 250 383 6804
email: info@trafford.com

The United Kingdom & Europe
phone: +44 (0)1865 722 113 ♦ local rate: 0845 230 9601
facsimile: +44 (0)1865 722 868 ♦ email: info.uk@trafford.com

10 9 8 7 6 5 4 3

Dedication

To Diana, Princess of Wales

"...and at length they pronounce'd that the Gods had order'd such things, thus more forgot that all deities reside in the human breast."

William Blake
"The Marriage of Heaven and Hell"

"Embrace Me, My Sweet Embraceable You"

Special Thanks To:

Carol DeMarinis for her beautiful oil portrait.
www.demarinisfineart.com

Todd Chandler for his masterful cover art and inventive photo montages capturing the essence of each chapter.
tchandlerdesign@gmail.com

Self-Realization Fellowship, Los Angeles California for the courtesy of allowing me to include the photo of Parmahansa Yogananda in Chapter 6 and the photo of the windmill at the Self-Realization Fellowship shrine in Chapter 30.

The National Park Service, Haleakala National Park, for the courtesy of allowing us to use Paul Rockwood's painting of "Maui Snaring the Sun," circa 1950, HALE 168 in Chapters 27 and 30.

Arthur Jackson, a leading popular music critic of the U.K.

Roger Donner, producer, *As Time Goes By*

Harry Warren, songwriter, *The More I See You,* his gift to both of us.

Michael Barr, songwriter and pianist.

David and Erin, wherever you are.

Part 1

Heaven Knows

Chapter 1

Richard

The first time I saw her I was leaning on a bar (where else?) at Jerry Van Dyke's in the Valley. She smiled at me, that beautiful smile. I couldn't take my eyes off her. She wore a light mink coat and black velvet pants. She looked right at me, with those green eyes dancing, maybe a little shy. My TV director, Thom, introduced us. I stayed next to her the rest of the evening.

I had never met anyone like her. After all, in the world I lived, as Dick Haymes, crooner, ballad singer, movie star of Technicolor musicals, women like her didn't exist, and if they did, I ignored them. I've changed since then.

Now that I'm dead.

I fell madly in love with her only to wind up pushing her away. I couldn't appreciate then what I know now. Once I was sure she loved me, I systematically did everything I could to destroy her love for me. I almost succeeded.

I can see her. She's grieving, of course, and all I can do

is sit here and watch. Once she felt me kiss her. But for the most part I have no way of easing her pain. I can only sit beside her helplessly and watch her agonize.

The only hell there is, is the one we make for ourselves. The only devil there is, is the one we let loose in ourselves. Well, I made my hell and I've let loose plenty of the devil in me and now I'm paying my dues. Not because I'm being punished. No way. We're loved, not punished. We're allowed to experience the results of our efforts, that's all.

I had my chance.

I was holding God in my arms and I didn't even know it, and now it's too late.

It will be a while before we can get together again, before I can hold her in my arms again and tell her how much I love her. I get the message to her, through her friends or strangers even. She's more open to me now that the evidence is so blatant. She's not censoring so much now that her grief is subsiding and all that psychology bullshit isn't interfering.

But it's not the same. Not like when I had her with me. When I lay next to her. I knew she wanted me to hold her (I always knew what she was thinking). I wouldn't.

She came to me every day, every morning and every night, except when she couldn't stand it any longer. Then she left town. And I slept through it. She seldom complained.

"At times when I am with you I feel like I'm not really there," she would say.

Funny, my other six wives made the same complaint. I didn't understand then. I do now. Now I've made a one hundred and eighty degree turn. Now I know how it feels to be there, to be ignored and unseen. That's what I mean by paying your dues. I had everything in the world at my feet for another, "comeback", as they call it, and this time with a woman who knew how to love—no conditions.

What did I do?

I devised every method I could to frustrate and test her. Always testing, testing, testing...

I couldn't believe it. She never gave up. She never let go. Yeah, she'd go away sometimes when she was hurting really bad, but she'd always come back. There was always another coming, half out of her mind with hurt and grief, but she'd come back.

She wrote on a photograph she gave me (I had pressured her for it), "I pray to God I will never betray the love I feel for you." And by God, she didn't. The only woman I ever knew who didn't, and I've known plenty, as everyone is well aware. No matter what I did, she'd look back at me with that quizzical look on her face, sort of sad.

"Richie," she'd say, "it doesn't seem to matter what you do, I never stop loving you."

Chapter 2

Keep it simple

Richard, you printed those words on all of your stationery, and boyishly tried to live up to them. Your celebrity status made your desire impossible.

I spent Christmas at the Coronado Hotel in San Diego this last week, the year of your death, 1980.

I went to the Prince of Wales bar named for your "father?" I never believed what your mother, Margaret, hinted at until I saw the photograph of the Duke of Windsor taken there in 1920. A year after your birth. He was a guest at the Coronado Hotel that year.

The picture is in profile. No two men could have a nose like that and not be related. His face is handsome, refined (like yours), the high cheekbones are the same, eyes slightly slanting upward, slightly protruding (like yours). But the nose, a small nose, tilted upwards, detracts from the otherwise masculine face. There is no longer any doubt in my mind that for once your mother was telling the truth. From your very conception, there was no way to keep your life simple.

February, 1979.

"Dianne, it's Susan. Thom asked me to call. We're filming a pilot for a new show. Come on over to Theta Cable in Santa Monica.

Dick Haymes is the MC. Wait 'til you hear him sing! Thom wants to do a face-over with you."

Sitting in my office in Beverly Hills, I listen as Susan, Thom Keith's girl Friday, tells me about the new show, *Hollywood Cabaret*. Thom Keith, writer/director of TV and movies liked to project my face over the singers he used in his TV shows to make them appear to be singing to me.

The year before, Thom and I met at a party in Newport Beach. Although we dated a few times, I backed off when I inadvertently walked into his house one morning. I found him in his pajamas surrounded by a bevy of Hollywood starlets in various stages of undress.

We remained friends out of our mutual interest in TV. I missed the days when I assisted Patrick Dennis, author of *Auntie Mame*, and producer of *Media Noche*, Channel 8, Mexico City.

I have just finished a therapy session with a client, an actress. Another child abuse victim. She regresses easily back to the age of five, then blanks out in screams of terror. At that moment, a visit to a television studio seems mercifully distracting.

"Sure, Susan, I'll be by about one. I'm leaving my office early and can stop at the studio on my way home. I have a new patient who insists on seeing me at my home in Santa Monica instead of, here, at my office."

I grab the jacket of my powder blue pantsuit as I hurry out into the blinding sunlight of Southern California and the chilly wind, brushing my long, auburn hair away from my face.

Thom is nowhere to be found when I arrive at Theta Cable.

"He's around. Try the food wagon," is all that my inquiries produce.

I wander through the studio until I find a door marked EXIT. Lunch is being served cafeteria style. Trays of sandwiches line the counters. Two young girls chat quietly at the front of the food van. In the back of the van, bent over, isolated in a corner, stands a white-haired man.

The name Dick Haymes does not mean much to me, although Susan's enthusiasm has aroused my curiosity. Could this man be the one she means? There is something about him that makes me think so. He seems totally unapproachable. I don't want him to think I'm staring, so picking up an egg sandwich, I walk away.

No, this person can't be the "Star." I remember vaguely at twelve seeing a movie called *State Fair*, with Jeanne Crain and one of my childhood heroes, Dana Andrews.

I was seated with Jeanne Crain and her husband at a charity ball two months ago, just before Christmas, still 1980. Allen Chase, founder of Who's Who International, had invited me. She was as beautiful as ever, but sadly overweight. I recall the words to the song that were dubbed for her, "It Might As Well Be Spring." I knew them by heart.

I remember Dick Haymes in that movie, but he had not interested me.

Could this white-haired man be the Dick Haymes?

Disappointed in the white hair, too old for me, still looking for Thom Keith, I rejoin the group in the studio. I pass by the piano. The white-haired man is talking in a low voice with the pianist. Something in the intensity of his words makes me stop and listen. He is going over and over the last few bars with the pianist. I admire his professionalism. This must be the famous Dick Haymes Susan was so excited about. I have lived my entire adult life outside of the United States with the exception of the last four years, in which I have buried myself in the academic world of clinicians to obtain a Ph.D. in psychology and a license to practice in California. My knowledge of the film industry and the music world is the little I glean from a caseload, including actors. Their problems are not dissimilar from anyone else's since, for the most part they are successful, but still suffer from the usual rejection which is a professional hazard for the undiscovered and, as I am soon to learn, the discovered.

Not finding Thom, I sit down in the *Cabaret* scene with the author of Redd Foxx's book, and another of Thom's cronies I have met several times at parties at the Sportsman's Lodge in Studio City. We are to be background audience for the show, only the water we are drinking has been replaced with pure vodka by Redd Foxx's author.

Thom appears on the set. "Take your places, everyone," he says. "The shooting will begin." Thom's voice is none too steady. His paisley scarf is askew. His brown hair is uncombed. His sports coat is wrinkled. He must have slept in it. I suppose he is drinking again. The proverbial countdown begins. Then Dick Haymes sings:

"It's a Grand Night For Singing..."

A perfect sound reaches my ears. I sit up straight in my chair, staring hard in the direction of the man producing those incredibly rich baritone notes, a perfect, unblocked, untraumatized sound.

For almost fifteen years I have been looking, searching for someone to love who can love me back in mind, in body, and in spirit. I have read in a Yoga book that a love based on these three levels is the greatest of all human experiences. Yet, I had given up any hope of finding someone with whom I can share this kind of love. At that moment in my handbag is an airplane ticket to London en route to Findhorn, Scotland. In lieu of finding this impossible dream, I plan to investigate the Findhorn Community established several years ago by Peter Caddy. At least living there I would be surrounded by people seeking spiritual union.

The words of Richard's song reach into the heart of me:

"Maybe it's only a dream."

But it is not a dream. He is standing there in front of the microphone. He is real. He is producing those sounds and no one could produce those sounds who is not in union with himself, who is not free of all armoring. I sit dumbfounded, inert and unbelieving, as my heart rises in a crescendo with the music.

"I think that I'm falling in love,

Falling, falling in love.”

The song ends.

I look at my watch. Frantically, I remember I have a new patient waiting for me. Lost in the music, I have completely forgotten.

“Cut,” Thom calls.

I jump up. “Thom, I’ve got to go.”

“Don’t. We haven’t done your face-over.”

“Another time. I’m late for an appointment.”

“Who’s she?” That voice, Richard’s rich baritone voice, rings out.

“A psychologist,” someone yells back.

“Tell her to stay. I could use one.”

“You can sit on my couch anytime,” I can’t believe I say that as I walk by him.

That is not my style. But I mean it and leave, never expecting to meet him again. I have forgotten that it is Valentine’s Day. I have also forgotten that when the gods want to punish you, they answer your prayers.

Chapter 3

The red light is flashing on my answering machine when I finish my last session the following day. The message is from Susan.

"Isn't he terrific! How would you like to see him again? He's having a party tonight at Jerry Van Dyke's in the Valley. Call Thom."

I call.

"Dianne, can you pick us up?" he asks. "My car's not functioning, and Susan's car has collapsed. Stop by the studio at seven."

When I pull open the door at Jerry Van Dyke's night club, I'm wearing a light mink coat, over an off-white shirt tucked into tight black velvet pants. My auburn hair hangs thick and full around my face...

Richard is sitting at the bar. He smiles at me. I smile back and slowly, trance-like walk toward him.

"What would you like to drink?" he asks. Our names seem irrelevant as he indicates a barstool for me to sit on next to him.

"A vodka tonic," I say, sliding onto the barstool without lifting my eyes from his face. Our eyes absorb each other. Thom, Susan, the nightclub itself fade into a backdrop of unreality. Only he and I are real.

He stays by my side the rest of the evening.

From the bar he escorts me to the dining-room where the entertainers are singing old favorites from the forties. Richard greets his guests. He is giving the party for the staff and cast members of *Hollywood Cabaret*. Whenever he has to leave me he excuses himself graciously and returns as soon as he can. So many people come over to see him, musicians, actors, people I do not know...people he does not know. Everyone wants to speak to him, but he always comes back to me. A performer at the club begins "Elmer's Tune," then sings "Moonlight Cocktails." I sing along with Richie (or Richard, his close friends do not call him "Dick"). He is amazed that I know the words.

As a youngster in Rocky River, Ohio, I learned the songs. Singing helped me assuage the loneliness I didn't know I felt. My Italian father sang and taught me songs, even older ones, from World War I. I can remember "Round Her Neck She Wore a Yellow Ribbon" and "The Caissons Go Rolling Along." I must have learned to sing when I learned to talk. I do not remember not singing. For me it is easier to sing than to talk, especially with a man who interests me. I do not know how shy I really am.

The drinks help. I am shaking inside, but I don't know it ... I feel exhilarated. When dinner ends, we move to another room where the disco music keeps up a beat for dancing on a small wooden platform. Thom asks me to dance.

"He likes you. He likes you a lot."

"Do you think so?" I ask, trying not to sound interested.

Somewhere inside me none of this information registers. I can't take it in. I can't even entertain the idea. This famous singer, this movie star can't be interested in me. I also know that the sensation I am feeling has little to do with his fame, his voice, and his celebrity status.

Thom and I dance well together. I hope Richard notices. We sit down. Richard asks if he can take me home.

"No," I say lamely, "I'm taking Thom and Susan home," wishing I weren't.

Richard persists. As we stand outside on the balcony before descending the stairs, again he asks me. And the third time I refuse.

"No, I really must take Thom and Susan home. I came with them." I am too shaken to say anything clever.

"He really likes you," Susan repeats Thom's words in the car, adding, "He's divine...what a voice! Do you know he was married to Rita Hayworth? Isn't he the most handsome man you ever saw?"

Some part of what Susan says begins to penetrate. I am accustomed to famous people, Patrick Dennis, introduced me to many, including Rosalind Russell. I even met the Presidents of Mexico when I lived there.

No, this is different. I am beginning to grasp the meaning of the word "celebrity," and the aura around this man that makes him so special. It was not just his voice, though it ought to have been.

Later, as I read the cover of Richard's latest album, "As Time Goes By," I am entranced by what Arthur Jackson, one of Britain's leading pop music critics, writes:

"Right here and now Dick Haymes is the world's supreme ballad singer...It was back in 1942 that I came under the spell of Dick's rich, baritone voice on the original Harry James 78's of 'My Silent Love,' 'I'll Get By,' and 'Old Man River.' He got full label credit, too, at a time when even Sinatra was still lurking coyly under the 'with vocal refrain by' on Dorsey record labels...Impossible to believe that Dick Haymes has been singing for close on 40 years. This is the voice and technique of a young man; except that no young performers of today could ever match Dick's lyrical phrasing, his intuitive musicianship, and warmth of tone..."

There was something special about him, as well as his voice. Something different that I had never known. I had "fallen in love" before, to use an old cliché, in high school, in college, and twice since my husband and I had separated in 1968 after sixteen years of semi-marriage. The attraction was always physical and intellectual, nothing more. Something was missing; perhaps something in me. As I began my training as a psychotherapist, I took seriously the biblical passage, "Physician, heal thyself."

"Dick Haymes just called." Thom phones me the next day. "He wants to know if it would be alright with me if he called you. He needed to know if we are going together. I said I'd check with you."

"Thom, he may call."

He hangs up and within 30 seconds, Richard is on my line. "I'd like to invite you to dinner tomorrow night," he says in that incredible voice.

"Oh, thank you, but I'm going to Oakland."

I could have accepted tomorrow. I could cancel my trip. Why did I say that? I'm holding onto my voice, so afraid I'll give myself away.

"When will you return?"

"Monday."

"Let's make it Tuesday."

"Yes, Tuesday."

...will be my good news day, I think, lyrically. I am not believing...this cannot be. How can a man who married the glamour queen of all time be interested in me? I breathe deeply as I think, *Tuesday is almost a week away.*

My daughter, Connie, who had recently graduated from Boalt School of Law, meets me at the Oakland airport and drives me to Helen Wambaugh's Dolphin Farm, a picturesque New England style, white frame house resting snugly atop a mountain overlooking green pastures, far from the sea and any dolphins. I have arranged with several colleagues to spend the weekend with Helen Wambaugh to learn more about her research in past life therapy and reincarnation.

Helen, author of *Life Before Life*, tabulated thousands of regressions of American people to demonstrate that they, contrary to popular opinion, remember living on farms in the midwest—ordinary, uneventful lives—not as kings and queens in Europe. Her tabulations match the population census of the past two hundred years in the United States.

Another observation Helen makes this weekend, one I am to remember vividly fourteen months later, is that forty percent of the people in the United States have personal experience communicating with dead friends and relatives.

All of this is new to me. My only interest is in helping my patients, one of whom has been relieved of a debilitating heart condition following the re-experiencing of a devastating fire in which her parents had lost their lives five hundred years ago. Her fiancé rescued her from the fire and held her back when she tried to rush in to save her parents. She screamed as she fought to free herself from his grip. Afterward her heart condition improved and she went back to work.

I do not believe nor disbelieve. If re-experiencing a past life will help a patient out of a trauma, what difference does it make whether the memory is accurate or not? The point is to get well and live a joyful life. I am attending the workshop to learn technique.

Helen demonstrates various methods, some of which are familiar to me. When my patients began flipping into previous life-times during regressions, I had sought out Morris Netherton, author of *Past-Life Therapy*, who regressed his patients by using an "operant phrase," which he would pick up from them when they were describing a present day traumatic event.

My personal regressions with him, I attributed to my vivid imagination. They were: loss of children, kidnapping, rape, death, rebirth and also a monotonous, laborious life on a farm in colonial America. I had no spontaneous emotional release.

Helen chooses me to demonstrate her methods. She uses guided imagery to take me from the beta or conscious level to the slower alpha frequency commonly known as a twilight zone.

I see nothing during Helen's countdown of the centuries until she arrives at a time several thousands of years before Christ. What I see resembles an ancient Mayan *tianguis* (a market place), but I know it is not Mexico. The scene reminds me of a regression I experienced with Bernadette McNulty.

I had met Bernadette, a striking, red haired beauty, struggling across the Mexico City International Airport Terminal, limping badly, half-carrying, half-dragging two small children, plus luggage. I stopped to help her. She suffered from muscular dystrophy. Suffer is not the best word to use because Bernadette refused to suffer. Her disease was a challenge to her. The children belonged to a fellow medical student. Bernadette was to deliver them to their grandparents in California.

When I saw her years later, contrary to a grim medical prognosis, she had reversed the symptoms. Her limp had improved. Since I had watched my favorite aunt slowly deteriorate with this disease, I was amazed.

In response to my expression Bernadette offered this explanation:

"Certain exercises, diet, vitamins, devised by a specialist in Pasadena and a prayer group that meets weekly in a Methodist Church in Sherman Oaks." Then she looked at me sharply. "I want you to regress me. I need to know why I have been given this affliction, or why I have chosen it. What have I done?"

I had learned from Rabbi Lerer with whom I had studied Hebrew in Mexico City that in Hebrew the word for "judge" is the same as the word for "teach." He explained that we are not judged; we are taught.

"It's not a question of punishment," I said to Bernadette, "perhaps more like a lesson."

Bernadette nodded her approval. "Then I need to understand the lesson."

In her regression, I discovered Bernardette had been a high priestess in Atlantis, not long before the island nation sank from view. She could heal people but she could also cause harm. For power and a price, she helped the Atlantean governor's daughter win back her husband with a love potion. The husband of the governor's daughter had left her for another woman.

Although I am unaware of them, Helen has gathered my fellow therapists around me as my mind journeys into a time past:

"I am seeing an ancient city square," I say aloud. A stepped-pyramid rises up in the center. A flame burns continuously at the top. A high priestess tends the flame. I am very young. I live in my widowed mother's house. She is angry with me. I am an embarrassment to her. I have a son by a married man who lives with us. A man I love desperately. My mother wants him to leave. One day, without warning, he goes back to his wife, the governor's daughter. He is Captain of the Governor's Guard.

"My mother is relieved. Our affair has been no secret to the Atlanteans, who do not approve. In my anguish, I flee to the pyramid, to the high priestess for help. Half way up the steps, I lose faith that she will help me. I fall on my dagger and collapse in a pool of blood. A young boy runs to find the Captain of the Guard. When he sees me on the steps, the pain he feels, the horror of finding me dead, turns to rage. The public spectacle I have created reflects on him. He wants to be the next governor. I move my hand to caress him. My hand passes through him. I cry out to him. I cannot penetrate his shield of anger. I realize I am dead. His grief is swallowed up in his humiliation. His love of power is greater than his love for me."

As Helen brings me back to the present time, I feel remorse and a deep sadness. I am impressed by the vividness of the recall. I could see the stone walls and atrium of the house in Atlantis where I lived. I could see the toga-like drapery of the gown my mother wore; the leather of the captain's uniform my lover wore. I felt how much I had loved him.

Then...I begin to have a strange feeling that somehow Richard is my lover in this story, the man I had loved so

much, a man I could not live without, a man of ambition,
a man I could no longer reach.

And I am to see him...

Tuesday.

"Haven't we met before in another lifetime?"

Chapter 4

Tuesday

"Dianne, your skirt needs pressing and your hair isn't combed," my roommate, Debbie, chides me.

I have just received my license to practice from the State of California in January, and rooming with Debbie eases the burden of rent. She is also good company, bright, vivacious, and practical. She plugs in the steam iron as I remove my skirt like a child obeying a mother's commands. Debbie is the age of my daughters, whom I miss. I am shaking so hard inside, I can feel it.

Richard is due to pick me up at 7:00.

Discarded clothes are strewn all over the bed. I finally choose a flared off-white wool skirt, matching turtle neck sweater, and coat with Dolman sleeves, high collar and full swing.

Debbie brushes my hair; it is soothing, but I am so nervous I wonder if I should call him and plead illness. I am worse than a teen-age school girl on prom night.

Richard arrives at exactly 7:00 PM. He wears a blue

denim hat, kind of cocky, a checked sport coat and slacks. When he walks in my living room he fills the entire space. Though slender in build and fine-boned, not quite six feet tall; he seems so imposing. I feel like I am in a dream, making a movie. I have the script, but haven't yet learned my lines.

This can't be actually happening.

I mumble, "Hello." He makes no move to kiss me or shake my hand.

He responds, "Shall we go?"

We walk across my patio, down the garden path, to his car, a brown Cadillac convertible of tank-like proportions, with brown leather seats. I slide in. He carefully opens and shuts the door for me,

I don't remember anything he says as we drive by the shimmering Pacific Ocean on our way to Malibu. Not until we are seated side by side at the restaurant, Trancas in Malibu—two candles glowing on the narrow table in the firelit dining room—do I remember the first words being spoken.

"Haven't we met before in another lifetime?" he casually asks me, as if he wants to know what kind of wine I like.

I freak.

We begin our dating at a series of brunches, lunches and dinners, every day for fourteen days. He never kisses me or moves to touch me except to take my arm when we are walking. He lives at the Century Wilshire Hotel in a suite of rooms, including a kitchen he never uses, near

Westwood Village. I don't see the kitchen until the fourteenth day.

The Century Wilshire is painted white with blue trim. Crystal chandeliers and gilded mirrors conflict with a modern exterior. Richard has made friends with everyone who works there, the bellhop, the desk clerk, and sometimes an out of town guest. He assiduously avoids the swimming pool.

We often walk to Westwood Village or to a movie. We talk and talk. He tells me about missing Malibu. He lived there with his last wife, Wendy, and their two children, Sean and Samantha. Sean has his own horse. Richard shows me pictures of his house and Sean riding the horse. Sean looks so much like him.

Richard will not show me pictures from his previous years, nor give me a reason why. He does not like to talk about his other glamorous wives: Joanne Dru, Rita Hayworth, Fran Jeffries, and Nora Eddington. The sixth, who is really the first, is nameless, a proposal of marriage based on a non-existent pregnancy followed by an annulment. I never knew her name. I don't think Richard remembered it either. He is not proud of so many marriages. He tells me about his fifteen years abroad in England and Spain. His Spanish accent is good. His French is excellent. He mentions his early school years in Paris and his terror of his French teachers. We have so much to say though none of it is very revealing. He is reserved and yet open and jovial.

I am never tongue-tied with him again. Just cautious.

He is forthright, natural. He responds politely to every stranger who speaks to him. He is recognized wherever we go, from a brunch at the Bel-Air Country Club, to Zucky's Deli in Santa Monica, to the Bicycle Shop, to Yesterdays, to The Old World, or a charming French restaurant. He is stopped anywhere, even while we are walking arm-in-arm down Wilshire. I enjoy the attention immensely, much more so than he does. The novelty never wears off.

On the fourteenth evening, casually, almost shyly, Richard asks, "Would you like to spend the night?"

Everything in my head says no. My mouth evidently is connected to my heart, because my mouth answers with a loud and clear, "Yes, I would."

"I don't know if I can make love."

"I'm not staying for you to perform. What happens, happens. I'm staying because I want to be with you."

He goes into the bedroom and lights some candles.

He pulls back the bed covers. I undress. He does not help me, nor watch. He mentions having lost some weight. He does look much too thin. We slide into bed together as though we have been doing just that every night for years.

Once in bed he kisses me for the first time on the mouth. His shyness – no, not shyness—his reserve falls away between the sheets.

Richard is number one in singing and number one in love-making. Not that he says so, but he wears a gold number one on a chain around his neck, a gift from a fan. He later asks me if anyone has ever made love to me better than he does.

I foolishly say, "Yes."

The man was not someone I loved, I quickly explain. It was the mood and the timing and the "grass," not the man.

Richard is the best lover, as well as the best ballad singer I have ever known. Making love for Richard is an art. As his body is an instrument for making those resonant baritone sounds, so response from my body reassures him that his artistry in making love is also number one.

In bed, I am first, always first. My need is his need. His selflessness is beyond measure. He gives and gives freely and willingly and joyfully. He helps me to know my body. *I become the body he sings through.* He knows better than I do when the final note is sung. He knows better than I do whether any dangling feeling of passion is not yet extinguished. He knows better than I do when the last vibration has been played out.

His pleasure becomes my pleasure, and when my satisfaction is so total that I can come no more, I slide between his legs and put my mouth with so much love between his legs. When his arousal is complete he enters me.

He holds me tightly crying out with joy, sobbing, "Dianne, Dianne, I love you, I love you, I love you."

I move in.

Chapter 5

Although I have successfully completed my licensing exam for the Board of Behavioral Science, I continue training. My mentor and teacher, Dr. Solon Samuels, recommends ongoing therapy for those of us pursuing a clinical career. He insists we become well-versed in five techniques including his own specialty, psychoanalytic psychotherapy. After Jung and Adler, I add Wilhelm Reich's and Alexander Lowen's bioenergetics. For the latter my trainer is David Howard. His regressive techniques are taking effect.

"I think I'm crazy," my remark to Dr. Samuels.

"What makes you think that?"

"I am remembering my brother-in-law and a friend of his, Dr. Rafael de la Fuente putting me in a mental institution. For thirty days I received electro-shock."

"First of all, you're not crazy. Second, that would be extremely excessive. On what grounds were you admitted?"

"I don't know. All I remember is my husband threatening my life, accusing me of adultery. It wasn't true, but he threatened to shoot me or lock me up in an insane asylum and take the children away from me. At least I felt safe in the hospital."

"What you describe is not correct medical procedure," Dr. Samuels says. "Was your brother-in-law a psychiatrist?"

"No, a gastroenterologist."

"Then he had no basis on which to admit you."

"I'm afraid to say this but I feel I was raped during those thirty days while I was unconscious."

"The electroshock could make you feel like you had been raped since you had no knowledge of it and had not given your permission for it. However, rape does happen in mental hospitals."

I begin an investigation, interviewing patients and caretakers. I question my colleagues, especially those who have completed their hours in psychiatric hospitals.

A patient discloses, "Oh yes. That happened regularly where I stayed. If I didn't agree to have sex with them, I'd still be there. It was the only way they would write a good report so I could get out."

Leslie Waldo, a friend and psychotherapist in private practice adds, "electroshock" to my investigation: "The doctors used it to punish patients into submission," he says. "It was horrible to watch. They couldn't just tie the patient down or they'd break the poor bastard's neck. They had to hold him. Disgusting, but there was nothing I could do to stop them."

In the middle of the night I wake up screaming. I

can't stop. I can't stop trembling. Richard wraps his arms around me, rocking me until I am calm enough to choke out the words.

"I am in a dream. I'm walking down a tree-lined sidewalk. I see my brother-in-law, coming toward me. I reach out my hand to shake hands with him. Instead, he throws me down on the ground and rapes me, leaving me in the gutter."

Richard says nothing, but holds me through the night until the shaking stops.

By morning, Richard begins to share his own experience of rape.

"In the forties in New York City, the police would form a human cordon to keep the crowds back so that I could enter the theater in the morning and leave at night. I would stay there all day. I couldn't leave between shows. I probably did six shows a day, and between shows I'd sign autographs. One night when I was coming out of the theater, five thousand screaming women broke through the police line. Before the police could stop them the women ripped off my clothes and even pulled out my pubic hair."

He understood about rape.

"I wish we had met when we were young, before any of this happened," I whispered to him.

"No, you wouldn't have liked me the way I was then, and I wouldn't have appreciated you."

"Maybe so. But it seems our previous lives, although pulling us together, are also pulling us apart."

I called Sunny Lash, my closest friend. She was for me the mother I never had. Together we could laugh away anything. For us, all insurmountable problems were hilarious.

I wanted Sunny to attend my next session with David Howard, the neo-Reichian therapist. The dream had been so real. In my previous sessions with David, I came out of the regressions, remembering nothing. I needed a witness.

The session began in the same way: ten minutes of rhythmic breathing, alternating eyes open wide, eyes clenched, while using my diaphragm for inhalation and exhalation,

"I am in Dr. de la Fuente's hospital," I begin. "It is evening. I am begging the female nurse not to leave. She promises me she will stay the night. I do not believe her. A male nurse comes in about nine p.m. I begin to feel drowsy from the injection he gives me. The male attendant is wheeling the gurney down a long dark hallway. I see nothing more. I am unconscious. A jolt of electricity runs through my head from right to left. Lights are flashing in my brain. My body convulses. Hands are holding me down. I am feeling a thrusting in my vagina. I try to lock my legs. I can't. They are tied to stirrups. I scream, yet no sound issues forth. I feel sexual impulses in my clitoris and vagina. I try to squeeze them, shut them off. I can't. With one last great effort, I scream, "Mario!" and lunge at my attackers. With nails extended like the claws of a tiger, I leap for his throat."

I regain consciousness. David Howard is disengaging me from his throat. Around me float feathers from the pillows he thrust in my hands. I have shredded them with my bare fingers.

I look at my friend, Sunny. "Tell me what happened," I ask.

"You appeared to me very frightened," she says. "You were moaning; your body was jerking. You were lying on your back, legs spread apart, knees bent. The forceful gyrations of your buttocks reminded me of a woman having sexual intercourse. Your body would convulse as though you had been drugged or undergoing electro-convulsive therapy, or both.

"When you came out of this, you looked exhausted; your face was contorted in agony, you stood on your knees, your hands looking like claws. You were screaming, 'I could kill you, Mario, with my bare hands for what you have done to me! How could you, how could you? What have I ever done to you? I trusted you!'

"I feel as though you have made a great breakthrough," Sunny added quietly.

I try to explain to myself as well as to David and Sunny what I am reliving, re-experiencing. "Sunny, the only Mario I know is Mario Brenes, one of the four medical doctors in the group of physicians surrounding my brother-in-law. I can't imagine he' would have anything to do with this violation. Why? What is the point? It's easier for me to pretend this never happened. I prefer to think of myself as insane rather than think friends or family members could even conceive of such a horrendous action. I have no frame of reference for being raped by someone I know."

Then I remember.

The graduating seniors, class of '48, Wagar Beach, Rocky River, Ohio. They had been drinking. Five of them attacked me, held me down on the sand.

I screamed, "Freddie! Make them stop!" He eventually did.

Axiom number one: what we repress, we repeat. My isolation defense stifled the shock of this memory for twenty-eight years. Again there were five, all well-known to me.

(Fortunately or unfortunately, I am an expert at denial.)

Chapter 6

Leaving my office one afternoon, skipping and singing my way across Santa Monica Boulevard in Beverly Hills to my car parked on Camden, feeling deliciously happy as I did those first three months in spite of my breakthrough in therapy, I see a Rolls Royce smash into another car near the Episcopal Church.

"Oh, my God!" I cry out. "He's hit a police car!"

The crowd bursts out laughing. Out of the Rolls jumps Dudley Moore on location for *Ten*. Director Blake Edwards praises Moore's accuracy and timing. They do not need to smash up the second Rolls, standing by in case the first "take" does not work.

"That is $40,000 you saved me." It is Blake's picture.

Richard is writing a screen play as well as his auto-biography. He takes it to his old friend, Blake Edwards, for suggestions. *Reprise*, as he calls the screenplay, tells the story of a broken-down alcoholic singer who is rescued by a young kid who wants to learn to sing. The singer stops drinking as he helps the young man learn. The young man becomes famous, then takes a nose-dive into drug rings and murder. The singer and a young girl who loves the young performer, attempt to rescue the new star. An ex-wife of the singer, also an alcoholic, enters the scene. Blake suggests Richard enlarge the ex-wife's part and bring her into the denouement. Of course, her name is Rita Hayworth.

Underneath my exuberance, a hollow feeling is tugging at me that is far from joyful.

"Oh, he's probably fallen in love with you because you remind him of Rita," a friend who knew her told me more than once. I am too deliriously happy to hurt, or give it credence.

"It's your hair," the friend continues. "She has auburn hair like yours."

I say nothing.

I finally acquiesce when Richard asks me to regress him so that he can remember his early life more clearly for the autobiography he is writing. I am hesitant to do it. I do not want our relationship to become one of patient and therapist. He insists in the same way that he asks me for my picture. I keep forgetting to give one to him. I still can't believe he loves me. Weeks go by before I give him my picture, or do the regressions. I am loathe to take control on center stage, for fear of losing him.

The two of us as housekeepers are unschooled, untrained and unknowledgeable. By eating out we save the kitchen. The hotel provides maid service, although I can make the king-size bed if I have to. I had been schooled out of housework by my husband who caught me ironing his shirts when we were first married and living in Mexico City.

"My Mother never ironed my Father's shirts!" My husband's booming voice had rattled the sterling silver bowls and trays on the buffets. "That's what servants are for."

I never ironed again, nor cooked, nor cleaned. The six servants did it. My only task was to oversee it.

Richard and I had a delicious meal of beef stew at a friend's house. Inspired by this stew, Richard and I decide we should save money and cook at home. We can't find a stew pot in our kitchen, so we go shopping to find a proper pot. Eventually we come across a large, heavy, black iron pot, eight inches high with a lid. It has the air of looking like it belonged to someone who can make another delicious beef stew. We buy vegetables and beef at the supermarket and proudly go home to put all of our ingredients together in the big black pot, which we fill to the brim with water. Our concoction boils away for most of the day, but continues to maintain its level of water and vegetables. The meat gets tougher and tougher.

We continue to eat out.

Richard continues on his screenplay, interviews biographers, calls his agent, and gives him "hell" for not coming up with some new gigs. I do therapy.

I wake up early, swim in the pool, and am gone before Richard wakes up. Between patients, I squeeze in meetings with his producers who have apparently run out of money. The television pilot is not picked up. Other people call for telethons or promotions.

The closeness and intimacy are difficult for me as my husband had seldom been home and had shared little of his life with me.

I have to go home. I don't know why.

I pull out of the hotel underground parking area onto Wilshire Boulevard, head for the 405 Freeway, move to the right, swing onto the 10, crying my way to Santa Monica. Then I'm back to Alta Avenue with its trees, real grass, magnolia blossoms not yet blooming, the ocean view, and my patio. Nature and my own things give me strength.

I phone. "Richie, this is me. I'm home. I'll be back in a few days. Something I have to get through by myself."

He understands. I love him so for that, no questions. Just...

"Come back when you can."

I sit there for three days reliving and releasing anger and grief. In part, it has to do with my father. I am special to my father, but he never listened to me. I always listened to him. He never once asked me how I felt or what my hopes and dreams were. It was like I did not exist. And now I am so much in focus, in Richard's focus. I am accustomed to being the wallpaper, and Richard is making me into a very prominent portrait hanging on his wall in the living room. He includes me in everything.

If his agent calls Richard and says, "Be at such-and-such a place for publicity reasons."

Richard answers, "If I don't bring Dianne, I don't go."

Mostly we don't go. With one exception. Shortly after we first met, he goes to a party in Santa Barbara without me, given by his friend, Robert Mitchum. Except for this one time, he never goes again, anywhere, without me. Maybe I am hurting Richard's career, but I am grateful he wants me to be with him.

I have not yet given him my photo. My passport picture is good. I have my local photographer blow it up.

In three days I am back with the picture. Richard is glad to see me.

We wash clothes at midnight, after watching *Benny Hill*. He knows Benny Hill, he knows everyone on television. Monday through Friday at 11:00 p.m. we laugh our way through Benny's antics until 11:30 p.m.

Watching the show, Richard says, "After visiting Benny in England, I was amazed at how this extrovert, who did almost everything for these shows, wrote the scripts and music; played the parts; worked on costumes; produced and owned the series outright, was so incredibly shy."

By midnight we are in the laundry room. Everything is dumped in together. I have never been accomplished at sorting and doing different loads. Richard thoughtfully adds a sheet of paper in the dryer to cut back on the electricity. Then we go back to television and watch *Small*, or is it *Short*, or *Get Smart*, that little man who worked for CONTROL but was generally a fuck-up. I suppose I should not use that word. Richard wouldn't approve. At least, he never speaks that way. He uses the slang from the industry, like, "Babe," or "wasted," meaning killed, which is new to me.

Together we lie in bed at night. Richard reads to me from the *Bhagavad-Gita*. Krishna in conflict. The conflict is not clear to me, but the melodious sound of Richard's voice and the beauty of the passages soothes me into a restful slumber.

I never ask him why he loves to read the "Gita" so much. I assume it is a lesson from his teacher and spiritual advisor, Paramahansa Yogananda, who at one point told Richard that he would not be able to evolve further as long as he was married to Nora Eddington, Errol Flynn's ex-wife, and Richard's fifth, I think.

"I followed Yogananda's suggestion and shed Nora," Richard confesses to me, "That was a mistake. She was a good cook."

Later I wonder to myself if his remark about Nora is a reflection on me. I actually know how to cook. At least enough to teach the maids, but I've never had any practice.

I read Richard's books written by his friend, U.S. Anderson, who speaks of remarkable spiritual experiences on Maui. I am deeply moved by Ulysses S. Anderson's encounters because I have had several experiences of my own. So has Richard.

"I was working at a club in Blackpool," Richard begins. "In England. Wendy and the children lived far away in the country. Once a week, on my one day off, I would drive there to see them, and come back the next day. Most of the time I spent driving. I was drinking heavily to keep going. One night a very bright light filled my room in the hotel where I stayed in Blackpool.

"'If you don't stop drinking, you will die!'" a voice called.

"I stopped drinking."

We're sitting side by side in the living room of his suite overlooking the swimming pool.

His sharing encourages my own.

"I am resting in my apartment in Westwood Village before I moved to Santa Monica," I say. "Late in the afternoon I am waiting for a patient. The phone rings. I sit up, and as I reach for it, I am aware the light rays of the sun are pouring through the window, commingling with the sound waves rising from the telephone, forming a screen made of dots like a Seurat painting. On the screen appears a woman, so beautiful I know I am not hallucinating. I could not imagine anyone this beautiful. No one on Earth has ever been that beautiful. I can see only her head and shoulders hovering above the phone. Her hair is light brown, arranged in a turn of the century, bouffant style. She looks young, maybe sixteen.

"She says nothing, then smiles at me and the room fills with a golden-silvery light expanding to encompass me. I feel waves of love, then peace and then joy flow through me.

"I feel every cell of my being connect to every other cell, and each of my cells connect to every part of the universe. I am aware of access to total knowledge. At that instant I can answer any question on any subject that mankind has ever posed; in mathematics, physics, chemistry, how the universe began, or...how it will end.

"I feel her love, an incredible love that we humans cannot even comprehend. The most rapturous, sexual experience cannot begin to compare with the joy of being in this light. I call out, 'Mother!' Yes! She resembles my mother except for her youth and her other-worldly beauty, per-haps my grandmother who died so young.

"Then I hear the phone, still ringing. I pick it up to stop the ringing. She and the light vanish. I am aware that there is a total absence of fear, that I have entered another universe. There is a total absence of any feeling that does not radiate love, joy, or peace. A peace unknown on this earth where we continually betray or are betrayed," I whis-per to myself as Richard wraps his arms around me in silence.

"May I never betray the love I feel for you today," I write on the photo I gave Richard.

Testing one, two, three.

Chapter 7

My introduction to the world of Hollywood celebrities is gradual, fortunately, and at first enjoyable. I have become accustomed to our being stopped on the street while walking down Wilshire to the Village, to the various restaurants we frequent. Everyone is delighted to see Dick Haymes and serve us, talk to us. The Maitre d's give us immediate seating and constant attention. For the first time, I begin to feel a part of Los Angeles, like I belonged.

In Mexico City, whenever I went out, I invariably ran into people I knew or who knew me. But in the three and a half years of residence in The City of Angels, that has happened only two or three times. Now it is a daily occurrence. We do not know them, but they know us. Not us. Him! For me, it was the same. I do not want to be the one. I like the second hand attention, the sense of belonging, but not the number one spot. For me, that spot is still much too dangerous.

Richard charms them all, the busboys, waitresses, managers, people on the street. He has a ready smile, listens carefully, jokes with the quick wit of his Irish ancestry, thanks to his mother, Margaret. Occasionally, we dine with friends of mine and again, the laughter. He loves me for it. I laugh out loud, without restraint, from deep within me. I lean into my guffaws with my whole body, my head thrown back.

"I love to hear you laugh," he repeats, much to my delight.

We visit his second daughter, Nugent, in Oxnard. He feels guilty at having left his children when they were so young, when he and Joanne Dru, in essence, his first wife, separated. The annulment didn't count. He did not want the divorce. But he had tormented Joanne one time too many.

He recounts, "We were Mr. and Mrs. Hollywood. The estate we owned in Encino had, at one time, belonged to Charlie Chaplin. It was known as the Country Club. I was coming home one day and, as usual, the house, gardens, and pool were jammed with people I didn't know, nor did I care to know. Then the daughter of a well-known producer accosted me.

"'Hey, Dick, when did you join the club?'

"I usually hid out in a sound room I had built for myself and my mistress, Music. There I could forget the onslaught outside. Occasionally Joanne would break in and literally beg me to go to bed with her. I wouldn't."

"I don't know why I wouldn't." Richard asked me more than told me. "I just wouldn't. We had an agreement. We would each do what we wanted as far as making love with someone else was concerned, as long as we were discreet.

I was thinking to myself as Richard was speaking that Los Angeles or Hollywood is so different from the world I knew. Mexico City and Cleveland, in spite of the difference in culture and language, were the same. Sexual freedom for women was unheard of. I listen to Richard in awe.

"When she was up north filming *Red River*, I got a call from Duke Wayne.

"'Richie, you'd better get up here. Your wife is making an ass of herself.'

"So I went, and she was, with two leading men, John Ireland and Montgomery Clift. I slugged her, made love to her, and went home."

I can see he is not pleased with himself.

"She was standing near the edge of the pool," he continues, "in a long, frothy dress with a big hat. Showing off in front of all those people I couldn't stand. I couldn't resist. I pushed her in the pool. She filed for divorce the next day. She took everything I had. I shouldn't have pushed her in the pool, I guess."

We drive to Oxnard, seventy-five miles north of Los Angeles, to look at sailing vessels. He wants to buy one to sail to Hawaii. We look at several luxury yachts, forty-five to sixty feet in length. The one he chooses has a large berth for two, and a semi-circular row of windows, not portholes, reminiscent of a pirate's vessel. We try out the bed. There is plenty of space.

He mumbles, "I'd like to live on it."

No way! I think, but say nothing. I also know enough

about sailing to never venture a trip to Hawaii alone with him. I am an adventurer but also a survivor. I am glad he doesn't have enough money to do more than just talk about ordering it.

I am grateful to meet Nugent, his daughter, in her early twenties. She wears no makeup. She is as down-to-earth as Richard. He is so fond of her and so proud of the way she has overcome the usual temptations of L.A. teenagers. She supports herself and her baby, asking for nothing. I encourage him to see his family. I miss mine.

My two daughters and son all live far from me; my youngest, Alexandra, in Mexico City; my oldest, Connie, in Berkeley; and my son, Javier, in Alaska. I want a family. He does too, except that he feels he does not have the right. It's as though he has not earned it.

We have lunch along the quay near the sailboats. I excuse myself so that he and Nugent can be alone together for a while.

The only personal invitations he accepts other than the time at Robert Mitchum's are those from Tom Cooper, a talented singer in his own right. Tom, like myself, is from the Midwest, medium height, good-looking, warm-hearted. He makes me feel at home immediately. Tom operates two theaters, Tiffany and The Vagabond, where he shows the classic films that people never tire of seeing.

On weekends, usually on a Saturday night, Tom invites Vivian Blaine, Kathryn Grayson, Mel Torme, Virginia O'Brien, Donald O'Connor and a smattering of industry oriented friends or professionals: directors, songwriters, and musicians. Many of the stars I have seen on screen while growing up in Ohio.

The only one I met previously is Mel Torme. I entertained him at my home in Mexico City while he was performing at the Camino Real Hotel. He had picked up the "Aztec Tango," so I gave him the quick cure, a simplistic solution of *grageas de carbon* (charcoal). He prefers not to remember me.

"Dianne, how long have you known Richie?" Vivan Blaine sitting beside me remarks rather than questions.

I remember her from *State Fair* as I answer. "Not long, since February." *In the movie Haymes falls for her*, I'm thinking.

"He is very much in love with you," a bombshell I am not prepared for. Her directness leaves me speechless. I am no longer the wallpaper or a decoration in Tom's livingroom. I see her eyes glow with kindness, almost tenderness. "You are very lucky," she finishes.

What I have been afraid to ask or speak, she has put into words for me.

I answer, "Yes, I am."

Tom first met Donald O'Connor in 1970 as a guest performer on Donald's television show. The evening we are introduced, Donald amuses us with skits and songs from his *Texaco Theater* shows which I have never seen.

"I sang two songs on your show and you raved about me," Tom reminds Donald. "It was so generous of you."

Tom has a knack for befriending stars, the ones who have never lost touch with that soft spot somewhere inside called "heart."

Tom's home is appropriately located high in the West Hollywood Hills with a panoramic view of the lights of Los Angeles visible through the glass floor-to-ceiling sliding doors leading to the terrace and city beyond. A living room wall becomes a vast screen for the movie projector beaming its light across the full length of the room, from the projector room beyond the stairwell. It is considered by Tom a distasteful breach of etiquette to interrupt the beam. One learns to crawl under.

We sit on the most uncomfortable of couches (two white leather and chrome seats) but they belonged to "Judy," a gift from *A Star is Born.* Tom had acquired them at Sid Luft's tragic auction. I shall never forget the morbid and the curious, pawing over Judy Garland's personal belongings. Her child-sized costumes, her doll-like spiked heels were too small for anyone to try on. For me, the sale desecrated her memory. I had been relieved to leave.

In Tom's house, where she is appreciated and revered, Judy's couches are appropriate. They blend with the art deco style and the dozens of pictorial volumes of cinematic history resting on the oversized, circular coffee table and bookshelves. The couches are at home here, a Hollywood shrine.

Donald O'Conner and Richard had both sung with Judy; Donald on *The Judy Garland Show,* and Richard had cut records with her, songs from his movie *The Shocking Miss Pilgrim.* Although Betty Grable was the female lead, her contract prohibited her from recording anywhere else except for her studio.

That evening the stories unfolded from Richard about

the boarding house in Hollywood where they lived, trying to make stardom and ends meet. Strangely enough, those who lived in that boarding house at that time all became stars.

"It was the only time I was truly happy," Richard recalls. "We never knew how we were going to pay the rent, but I knew I would make it. We all did. We were having so much fun together. It was like a big family. I was doing stunts in those days. I dove from a one hundred foot mast. No insurance. No unions. But for a hundred bucks, I could live another month. It's a wonder I wasn't killed, but none of us thought about it. We were too busy making it."

On the way home, I questioned Richard about being happy.

"Not really."

"You mean in those days when you were so famous and so rich, making $65,000 a week back when money was worth something, and you were sailing around the Mediterranean with Errol Flynn on that hundred and ten foot yacht, you weren't happy?" This is difficult for me to comprehend.

"First of all the IRS took ninety percent of the money. But most of all I never knew if I'd have another job, another film.

I was playing hard to get by hanging out with Flynn. Either I'd get fired or get a larger piece of the action. I never relaxed. I couldn't enjoy it."

I was beginning to understand Hollywood.

Another evening at Tom's.

Dick Jordan, a publicist at Disney, and I are the admiring spectators when Tom and guests gather around songwriter Michael Barr at the piano to sing the old familiar show tunes. At times, I would get up enough nerve to sing with them.

This particular evening, Richard's agent, after hearing me sing, drops his usual rancor toward me for not being famous, therefore without PR value, and exclaims, "My God, she can sing! We should book her, too."

Those were the days when I first knew Richard and I'm flying high in a whole new world.

"If you've never been in love,
And you're longing for the
Happiness it brings,
Try your wings..."

Those are the lyrics of a song written by Michael Barr. Michael loves my husky voice, and I love trying my wings.

Chapter 8

In March for the first time I watch Richard perform in public at a telethon in the Century City Plaza, a highly successful, yearly affair for the animal shelter. I had heard him sing and MC on *Hollywood Cabaret*, but filming in a studio is not the same as a live public performance.

Musicians have a special radiance all their own. I am to experience this phenomenon when I meet three of the great band leaders with whom Richard sang: Ray Anthony, Les Brown, and Harry James. These are the professionals, the men and their music. They cut records straight through, no stops.

Richard chooses "Memories," after asking my advice, which I didn't give. I think it too slow and too sad for a one-song performance, but he is in that world of memories. He sang it beautifully for his last album *As Time Goes By*. I do not yet realize what this choice means and what *Reprise* means until he begins to sing in that open air plaza.

Earlier in the day we met with Ray Anthony, who is the band leader for the telethon. A few magic words whispered to each other is all the rehearsal they need. Time does not separate these musicians. Time for them is a rest between bars. Without missing a beat their musical language continues to flow when they meet again. The lapse of time does not exist.

The telethon tables and guests are outside in the vast open space of the plaza surrounded by three tiers of shops, nightclubs, restaurants, and theaters. To one side, under the cover of a makeshift tent, the technical people are testing equipment.

Richard asks me to sit inside the tent and watch him on the monitor. I say no. I want to see him perform. But something more than that compels me to stand in the cold air among the jostling crowd. I attempt to avoid the ground wires and cords entangled in a web which surround the microphone and lead to the masses of cameras and lights that turn the darkness into day.

I am so preoccupied with the anxiety I am feeling, I don't notice who is sitting at the table next to me. Gregory Peck, Jack Klugman and other famous people are taking calls for donations. I am not aware of anything except the mounting anxiety I feel, almost like I am going on stage. I feel the way I did before I sang in charity shows in Mexico City with my Junior League colleagues. I always had performance anxiety before my entrance. This was different.

For the first time since I met him, I see Richard standing alone, frail and thin, holding that microphone. The night wind swirling through the plaza could have lifted him like a leaf and swept him away from the crowd of spectators, camera men, technicians and Animal Shelter

staff. I pray to God to give him strength as he sings:
"Memories, misty water-colored memories,
In the corner of my mind..."
When the first deep baritone notes emanate from this fragile source, I calm down. I relax and breathe again as the sound of his amplified voice is carried to me by the March wind.

I am glad when it is over. Gregory Peck and Jack Klugman greet Richard and me. Richard is back in his element, the smooth, devil-may-care, high spirited self that I learn is the image he presents to the public.

Memories is totally out of context.

Our next public appearance has me in front of the cameras. Marvin Paige, a guest we met at Tom Cooper's has arranged a special Hollywood Awards Night. Marvin is a casting director on one popular daytime show.

The Beverly Hilton where Santa Monica and Wilshire Boulevards intersect is the scene for the awards. We are invited for dinner, a formal affair. Richard's perfect timing keeps us waiting until the final moment. "Better to be among the last ones in, and run," he explains.

I find out what he means quickly enough when the valet takes his convertible at the foyer of the Hilton. Fans are lined up on either side of the entrance to the ballroom. Richard grabs my hand and we begin to run down the center. (My mind flashes on *For Whom the Bell Tolls*, when the prisoner ran between two lines of people beating him.) Instead of clubs, light bulbs and cameras click on and off. A scream rises like a roar through the crowd as Richard is recognized.

We arrive breathless from our hundred yard dash to the safety of a cocktail lounge where the begowned and tuxed stars wait their turn to be introduced on television and to the guests at the banquet. We look about us.

"It isn't as elegant as what you are used to, is it?" Richard says.

"No, it's not." I am clearly surprised.

The cut, the style, the peau de soie, the jewels, and the coiffeurs of the women in Mexico City are far more elegant. Richard perceives my thoughts correctly. At times I think he knows me better than I know myself.

"What's her name? What's her name?" A woman cries out.

A panic stricken voice from the MC's assistant reaches my ears seconds before I grasp that the woman is looking at me.

Someone pushes me and there I am on television with all the glaring lights and cameras staring at me. And no name!

The MC tries to cover, "And this...and this..."

The assistant looks at him from off camera and shrugs her shoulders.

"This is the beautiful young lady," the MC continues gallantly, "that Dick Haymes has brought this evening. And here's Mr. Haymes himself, coming up right behind her."

I laugh, grateful, for the "young lady." From then on I carry cards with my name in large legible letters.

A maitre'd leads us to our table near the stage. Already

seated on my left is a man I don't recognize, accompanied by is a woman with a young boy.

"Who is that seated next to you?" Richard nudges me at the table.

"I don't know," I whisper back. "I don't think he speaks English. He doesn't seem to understand what I'm saying. He's speaking Italian to the lady and little boy next to him."

Richard is having a lively conversation with the actor on his right who played the overseer from *Gone With the Wind*. The back of my chair is bumping into Louise Thatcher, the horrid nurse from *One Flew Over the Cuckoo's Nest*, and Glenn Ford, one of my childhood favorites. Ford and Thatcher seem very much in love. I try not to stare in their direction.

So many of the stars from my youth are there. I especially remember Jack Haley who played the Tin Man in *The Wizard of Oz*. (How glad I am that he is given an award tonight. I read three days later in the *L.A. Times*, that he died.)

Richard is called to the stage to present an award to Vivian Blaine. He praises the colorful, upbeat musicals of the 40's and 50's, and her participation in them.

I am still not getting any more response than an occasional grunt from the non-English speaking guest to my left. Richard returns from the stage and pokes me again.

"No capisco." I gesture with my hands, feigning despair.

At that moment the MC is lauding a new young actor who has forged his way into prominence with his outstanding performance in *The Deer Hunter*. Richard and I have avoided the movie because of the alleged violence it contains.

The MC's voice rises to a crescendo. "Will Robert De Niro please come to the stage. Robert De Niro!"

The applause deafens our ears, and to my astonishment, my non-English speaking dinner partner stands up, walks to the stage, and accepts his award. Richard and I choke with laughter.

The waiter arrives with a bill for the dinner.

"There must be a mistake, we were invited," Richard jokes as he scrawls his distinctive autograph across the bill.

We are stopped again by fans before we can reach the valet parking. At least an hour passes as we press our way through the throngs of people demanding autographs. With each signature, we gain another yard. Someone whom Richie vaguely knows brings us drinks, making the trek more festive. I am elated. I love it! The lights, the excitement, the crowds screaming at us, cheering us. It doesn't matter in the least that I am not the celebrity. They act as if I were, and that is enough for me to shine, and sign autographs as people shoved pens into my hand.

At last I can understand what Richard means when he says, "In the early days we were Royalty. We were the Kings and Queens that the Americans didn't have but so deeply wanted."

Chapter 9

"I'd better start writing my autobiography while I'm waiting for that stupid agent of mine to find me a gig."

We're at home in Marina del Rey.

Richard slams the phone down. His attitude toward his agent is generally negative. I wonder why he keeps him on. He is not all that bad, just another frustrated singer and pianist turned agent. He brings a side of Richard to the surface I do not want to see, a need for a whipping boy. My husband had that same need, only I was "it."

"You'd better regress me so I can get this book started," Richard tells me. "Keep it simple. Start from the beginning and move forward chronologically."

He does not give me a chance to say no. We make an outline. Then we begin with some bioenergetics exercises. I use bioenergetics rather than hypnosis. The body does not lie, only the mouth does.

Richard never goes on stage (even though he might sing only one song) without tuning up his body with Yoga and vocalizing exercises for three hours. He never allows anyone to hear him practice, so I have to leave the apartment while he prepares. His Yoga facilitates the bioenergetics.

On the first try, he does not regress all the way back to his birth.

"I'm three years old, or very young," he begins. "I'm in Argentina on a farm. I love my father. He reads to me, poetry and stories. He likes me a lot. He's holding me on his lap. My mother is arguing with him. Money ... things aren't going well. We go on a trip. We're on a train. We go to Brazil. My father says goodbye to me. He hugs me and he's crying."

Tears stream down Richard's face. I bring him out of it slowly. He is so still I touch him to make sure he is alive. When he opens his eyes he looks at me strangely and holds my hand.

"I didn't know I cared about my father," he murmurs. "I haven't seen him since I was five. He tried to see me once when I was an adult, but I never responded. I didn't know I love him."

He holds me close. He's barely breathing. He needs my strength.

"My mother took me to New York," he continues. "She had a lot of men friends. I always felt that she cheated them somehow, like they weren't getting what they wanted. When they came to call, she'd have me meet them and she'd encourage me to sing and dance for them. She taught me to sing.

"There was one man in particular, a general by profession. He was there a lot. In fact he helped her set up dress shops, you know, exclusive couture clothes—in New York,

Paris and London.

"She gave concerts too, singing. We always lived well. Even when the crash came in '29 and all of her shops closed, we still lived well. When I wasn't in boarding school, I played with our chauffeur. I learned about cars, engines and driving.

"Mother got my father up to New York on some sort of business pretext that she and the general cooked up. My father wasn't there too long before he guessed why he was really there. His presence was necessary to cover for the birth of my brother Bob. I think Bob's father was really the general. I'm not too sure who mine is. I don't think Mac Hamish was really my father either. Margaret, my mother, used to hint that my father was someone very important, someone extremely well-known. Then she'd deny it. You could never believe anything she'd say."

Richard is barely conscious, immobile, lying on the bed. I am beside him, leaning over him to catch his words.

"My father left, returned to Argentina. He refused to give her a divorce. We went to live in Paris. I was terrified of the French mademoiselles who taught us. They were so strict. Everything had to be perfect. Every line had to be perfect. No mistakes. 'You've got to do your homework.'" This referred to his three hours working out before he performs. Richard deplores the abusive way Sinatra handles his voice, taping shows in his jacuzzi while drinking.

I thought to myself, no wonder he is such a perfectionist! His clothes are immaculate, always in order, hung properly, his shoes lined up under his clothes. His taste is impeccable, never ostentatious. His tux (his work uniform, he calls it) is never black, but a dark, dark navy blue. "The dark blue looks better under the lights," he explains.

"Back from Paris," Richard continues, "my brother, Bob and I, were sent to a military school in upstate New York. We'd been to school in Switzerland, too.

"It was so frightening sometimes. Margaret would forget to pick us up when there were vacations. One time in Switzerland a head master had to stay with us for three days until she came. So when I arrived at the school in New York, I'd run away to find her. I'd find her in a hotel in New York City.

"It was hard for my little brother, getting adjusted. His English wasn't good. In fact it was nonexistent. The other boys would tease us for not being Americans, and Bob would say, *'Mais je ne comprends pas. Je suis Americain.'* I am an American."

We both laugh. Richard's imitation of a young American, French-speaking child, is perfect. He has a great gift for mimicry and often makes me laugh by suddenly becoming Cary Grant or some other prominent personality.

"I began singing," Richard resumes more relaxed, "at a country club near where we lived in Connecticut. By then we didn't have much money, so I went to work doing the only thing I knew how to do. I was always good at sports, especially swimming, but there wasn't any money in that. So I went to New York to Radio City Music Hall and got myself a job as a page, sometimes as a messenger boy. Then I discovered the symphony was a few floors down, so I'd sneak down to listen to them rehearse. I got fired for that.

"I was writing songs and my friend, George Simon—you'll meet him soon, he's coming from New York to push his book *Music In America*—gave me an intro to Harry James. I went over to see Harry to sing one of my songs. He said he didn't want the song, but he could use a singer. That's how my career began. Harry gave me my first break."

That's enough for one day. There are so many people, six wives, six children, six grandchildren. Six. A lot to remember. He would chide me for not remembering all of his different friends, but I can only keep up with the ones I meet.

Other than Tom Cooper's parties, he accepted only invitations for publicity reasons. The next invitation that arrived came from Columbia Studios.

Rita's studio.

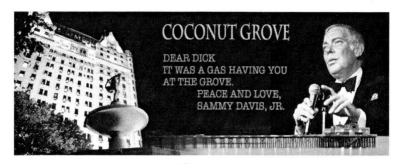

Chapter 10

April 1979

Columbia was Rita Hayworth's Studio; Twentieth Century Fox was Richard's. He had been the number two box office attraction at Twentieth Century back in the forties. Rita was number one, for Harry Cohn, the head of Columbia.

Before the date for the invitation at Columbia, Tom Cooper invited MGM's stars of yesteryear to a celebration at the Vagabond Theater. Although Richard's studio is Fox, he is legitimately invited for his performance in *Du Barry Was a Lady*, MGM, 1943.

The "running of the gauntlet" scene at the Hilton is repeated. The fans, even more prepared than at the Hilton, block us going into the theater. They have old photos of Richard for sale, ones he can't remember having ever seen. But he will not buy them. I want them, but my evening purse doesn't hold a checkbook. Again, I sign autographs. The crowd at the downtown Wilshire district, where the Vagabond is located, is definitely more perspicacious.

They suspiciously ask, "Who are you?"

"I'm a psychotherapist," I answer.

I am not certain that psychotherapist met their criteria of celebritude, but I look glamorous enough in my long fluffy, pale yellow gown. I wear my auburn hair tied up in curls which cascade down my back; topaz earrings dangle through the curls. I drag my mink behind me.

"Sign anyway," the fans say tersely.

I hope I am famous one day so that their efforts will not have been in vain.

After the film, *The Great Waltz,* the Stars and press go to Tom's home for an afterparty. Margaret O'Brien, Jane Withers, Marsha Hunt, along with Miliza Korjus, one of the stars of *The Great Waltz,* expand the usual guest list. Miliza's great operatic voice soon fills Tom's living-room. Even Richard joins in the song fest with Kathryn Grayson. Michael Barr is at the piano.

Margaret O'Brien still maintains that fey, elf-like quality at fifty. Sitting there, on Judy's white couch, she chats with me about films with the same wistfully soulful eyes and voice that endeared her to audiences when she was a child star. I think to myself, how she must miss that world. I wonder if Richard misses...I decide to ask him later.

Marsha Hunt's husband, Robert Presnell, is there and says he has just finished a TV play about Marie Antoinette. I tell him about my visit to Versailles, and the deja-vu I sensed as I twirled down the hall of mirrors and crystal chandeliers. At the Petit Trianon, the experience heightened when the guide pushed a secret panel, revealing a small room where Marie Antoinette would meet her lover, the Swedish Count Bernadotte.

"I felt I had been there before," I reminisce. "But I'm sure I was not she."

"Quite the contrary," Presnell responds, "you could very well have been. You have the same graceful movements and regal bearing she certainly had.'"

Sixteen years of verbal abuse from my husband had damaged me more than I knew. Presnell's words heal my sore spirit.

At the party the photographers snap me along with the stars. I am beginning to feel like one.

The pressure from the unaccustomed focus of so many people prick my memory.

"Beauty is only skin deep," my mother had admonished me severely as a child. "Handsome is, as handsome does."

Her words always clouded the screen on which I saw myself. I thought I am plain, freckled, colorless. I avoided mirrors. Later, my colleagues in psychotherapy training didn't believe me when I said that I didn't think of myself as beautiful. Only in unexpected moments when I am suddenly confronted with a mirror, can I see the glamour they apparently could see.

With a start, I return to the present, looking about for Richard. He is being stand-offish, hiding out on the terrace.

With a frown he says, "I never liked parties I was forced to attend, to keep the studio and Louella Parsons happy."

I think, *he's so much like Margaret O'Brien. Just as shy and wistful, only he hides it behind his jokes and savoir-faire. He never lets anyone see how vulnerable he is.*

Richard abhors publicity. *The Hollywood Reporter* and *Variety* have begun to call us at home. I ask them to please remember that we are "just friends," since neither of us are divorced. My puritanical Protestant upbringing controls me still. Fear of my husband's threats, even though we are separated, needle me. Mostly, though, Richard's need for privacy keeps me from saying what I am really feeling—that I love him. Blurbs about us appear, but kind ones.

In the afternoon before the Columbia Studio's reception, we receive a call.

"Please do not come," the voice says.

Richard graciously puts the caller at ease. "It would be no inconvenience for us."

"We are terribly sorry, but Miss Hayworth has refused to come if you do."

I am livid.

Richard and I have worked hard to bring rapprochement between Rita and him. To do that, I have regressed Richard again.

"I wish I could remember the last time we were together," Richard mutters, "but I was too drunk. I passed out. The day I married Rita, Orson Welles sent me a telegram that read simply, DON'T! He was right.

"She was so jealous that if I didn't make love to her every day she would accuse me of cheating on her. She was loyal though. Which is more than the rest of my wives were.

"She never asked for anything, but I went broke picking up the bills. We were shut up in a suite at the Plaza Hotel in New York for three months with the press staked out around us. We couldn't move.

"Harry Cohen was trying to have me thrown out of the country. Harry was afraid he'd lose his Star. He had the FBI after me. It took an Act of Congress to clear me.

"I was accused of being a draft dodger during the war. It wasn't true. I tried to enlist in the Navy and they wouldn't take me. High blood pressure. I wasn't even an American citizen. I'm still not. But I tried to enlist anyway. I love America. I did what I could, shows, the Hollywood Canteen...

"And all that time I was holed up in the Plaza with Rita. The money was pouring out. Thousands of dollars a day on maids, dogs, hair-dressers. I went broke. But she stuck by me.

"When we were living in Malibu, we had some good moments. I used to wash her hair, play in the shower, make love."

The muscles in my body tense. My fears return. I do not want to hear this. I feel so inadequate next to her. I have wanted to be playful, but he has always backed off ... except in bed. Then, and only then, do I feel loved. The rest of the time I feel like a good friend. I envy Rita.

"But then the arguments would start," Richard goes on. "She actually knifed me in the back once. Why do think she did that?

"What had you said to her?"

"All I said was that she couldn't dance."

"My God, Richie, that's all she could do."

What I should have said as a professional therapist was, "Why do you think that statement would upset her?" I never saw her in a movie until much later. That's when I realized that she could act too.

"We drank too much," Richard acknowledges. "Both of us. But she helped me. I was making a big come-back at the Coconut Grove. Everybody who was anybody was there, thanks to her. It was a tremendous success. Afterward, there was a big party in the hotel suite where we were staying. Again, we drank too much. All I can remember is that I was alone in the bedroom with her.

"'Now that you're successful again,' she told me, 'you won't be needing me. I suppose you'll leave me.'

"In my drunken stupor, I mustered the strength to hit her as hard as I could and then I passed out. I remember nothing more until morning. I woke up on the floor where I fell. She was gone. I got in my car and drove to our home in Malibu. She wasn't there, either. I called everywhere. No trace of her. I had bought her a new Cadillac. It was left standing on the street. She wouldn't take my calls. Three months later, she called me.

"'Where the hell have you been?' I demanded.

"She slammed the receiver down. I never heard from her again. That's twenty-five years ago? It feels like yesterday."

Thoughts race through my head. *Does he really love me? Is it true what so many people have said, that I must remind him of Rita?* I torture myself with the thought that, in his mind, I am only a projection of Rita on the silver screen of his mind.

71

Perhaps if he could see her, let her know how much he appreciated what she had done for him, he could assuage his guilt and end the memory.

"Since she won't see you," I suggest, "why don't you write her a letter?"

"She won't read it."

"If you give it to her at the party, maybe she will."

Richard had already written the letter. I want to go anyway, just to deliver the letter. But he will not hear of it.

I try to think of something. "Richie, now that we can't go, send someone else with the letter."

"She'll just tear it up or not accept it."

"At least try."

He will not. Tears come into my eyes. In my mind I can hear the strains of music playing the songs he sings so well.

"Last night when we were young ...
Ages ago, last night.

He cannot end it.

Chapter 11

I avoid thinking about Rita.

I am still under the spell of excitement and novelty. I avoid remembering what Richard said before we became lovers.

"I can't be faithful. I need more than one woman." This is said in response to my ideas on fidelity.

I ignore the warning. Oh, God, I love him so. We are together. Nothing else matters. What I have longed for since I read the words in the Yoga book is happening, love on all levels. I am uncomfortable about our marital situation and more so now about what the publicity might reveal. What a prude I still am!

Had not Saint Paul himself said when questioned about the ritual of marriage, "Once you have intercourse, you are married."

I begin to feel a presence in our suite.
"Richie, do you sense someone here?"
"Yes."
"It feels like..."

"Like what?"

"Like Betty Grable! But how could it be?" I try to laugh. Maybe I've been seeing too many of your movies."

"Betty's here a lot."

"But...but hasn't she died?"

"Yes!"

Her being there did not seem unreal to me, perhaps because I had seen my father several times after his death.

(Once, after his death, my father was waiting for me at the Cleveland Hopkins Airport. Another time I saw him while I was waiting for my sister at Saks, in Beverly Hills. And yet a third time in a dream. In the dream he took me to a reception desk where we signed in. Then we entered an elevator and rode up to a higher floor. We walked out onto a gray, barren land resembling a war zone after a bombing raid. A few stumps of trees remained. I learn later the full meaning. My father's appearances gave me support and nurturance, a commodity lacking in my childhood. A commodity I did not know I needed, since I had never experienced it.)

Since Richard and I both sense Betty's presence simultaneously, I do not question her being there. On the contrary, I accept her as a welcome ally. Betty is a supportive essence to have with us.

"We have been great friends." Richard liked having Betty there, too. "But she wouldn't let me visit her in the hospital when she was dying of cancer. I could only talk to her by phone. She said she wanted me to remember her as she used to be, not emaciated with cancer. I would have had an affair with her if she hadn't been Harry James' wife.

It would have spoiled my friendship with Harry."

Many people, not just Betty, appear at the foot of our bed. I see them as shadows, but Richard sees them clearly. John "Duke" Wayne, recently dead, is among them. All are from Richard's Hollywood history. Errol Flynn does not come to our bedroom.

"I saw him once across the street," Richard confides. "He beckoned to me. He smiled. I didn't accept the invitation."

At night after making love, Richard reads to me from the *Bhagavad-Gita*. Or sometimes from *Forever*, that charming story of two people in love in heaven, meeting again as adults, after their birth on earth. They have led separate lives in different parts of the world and then find each other one day at a ski resort, romance the night away with the intention to return to their own lives. Each die the next morning: he in an avalanche; she in an automobile accident. Touching.

After reading, and as Richard is falling asleep, he mentions the movies he is seeing in his head. Not movies that have ever been made—new ones. We seem to live many lives all at once. Avoiding the real one is the game we play.

"The Masquerade" Richard sings.

George Simon, Richard's old friend from New York, calls to say The Doubleday Company has invited book sellers across the nation to come for a celebration. He wants Richard to sing a number with The Les Brown

Orchestra. A film of American music is to be presented. We arrive at the Bonaventure Hotel. The darkened ballroom is filled with dinner guests when we slip in. Richard whispers a few words with Les Brown to prepare for his number. The last clip will be Les Brown playing, with Dick Haymes singing in synchronicity with the film clip. Richard will walk out of the screen at that moment, wearing the same clothes. Very effective. No rehearsal. Just do it.

As I watch, I am reminded of a story Richard told me.

"I was on a set with John Huston. That's how I learned to act, by observing. Tony Perkins is having a hard time with his lines, holding up the shooting.

"'I can't get the motivation,' Tony said in frustration. 'I can't get the feel of it.'

"'The only motivation you need'—Huston abruptly turned around and answered—'is your paycheck!'"

The ballroom is immense. At one end is the large projection screen from which Richard will emerge. The dinner tables surround the extensive dance floor. The band is playing. The words of the music come to me.

It's very clear
Our love is here to stay.
Not for a year
But ever and a day.

Richard takes me in his arms and repeats them to me in time with the music as we step onto the dance floor, unnoticed, the only opportunity we ever have to dance together.

George Simon introduces us to the other guests seated at one of the tables. I take my seat. A thousand people have begun dinner at similar round tables seating eight to ten people. Richard goes back stage. He never eats before a performance. The lights are lowered.

I have hardly begun to pick up my fork when behind me, Les Brown unexpectedly begins whispering to me. I turn but can barely see his face in the dark. The spotlight is now on George Simon.

Les says, "I can't tell you how glad I am that Richard has found you—found a lady at last."

Before I can speak, Les disappears into the wings of the stage near our table.

The movie begins. George's voice is amplified across the ballroom. His words add to the history of the various scenes of *The Music of America*, his book and film.

How could Les have known about us? I think. *How strange these musicians are. They seldom see each other, only when working together. They rarely speak. And yet Les knows more about Richard and me than we do, with those few simple words — found a lady.*

In the same darkness, a gentleman comes up behind me.

"You're the one who has saved Richie," the stranger says softly. "Stopped him from drinking. Bless you."

Again, I am astonished. Before I can answer, he vanishes. Les Brown and his band now appear. It is a film clip of a performance with Haymes singing, "Heaven Knows,

Anything Goes," a song made famous by Ethel Mermon in 1933. Cole Porter, the composer, is Richard's favorite.

Richard walks out of the screen without missing a beat or a word. Synchronicity. That is the word for musicians. Together, they add the dimension of synchronicity to life. Telepathy, clairvoyance, precognition, all are part of it.

"Words get in the way." How often Richard said or sang this. No masquerade among musicians. "Keep it simple."

I am beginning to understand what he means.

As he sings, the guests stop rattling their dinner ware. Slowly people stand up, as if hypnotized, walking trance-like toward the dance floor. They glide into the swing step, moving closer and closer around Dick Haymes. They pack themselves in, swaying in tempo. He ends on a long, rich-ly drawn out note that sweeps into the depth of all our souls, as far as eternity. The silence breaks with a burst of applause and cheers. I understand what has kept Dick Haymes in the limelight for forty years.

Chapter 12

Richard calls. "Tom's asked us over. He has a surprise. I'll pick you up in a half hour." He hangs up the phone.

Time enough to change. I am back at Alta Avenue in Santa Monica, where most of my belongings reside without me, and where I occasionally go to see a client when not using my office in Beverly Hills.

I pull on a sweater. The off shore breeze chills the early evening air. Should I switch on the heat? No. Richard will be arriving shortly. He is always on time. There's still some daylight. With a sweater I am warm enough. What will it be tonight? Tom promised a surprise. Maybe one of Richard's films I have yet to see.

Tom's friend, George Crittenton, admires Dick Haymes. Crittendon works at Films Inc., the distributor for Fox movies which are not to be exhibited in theaters. Therefore, he is able to bring 16 mm prints of Richard's movies for screenings at Tom's house.

At 7:30 promptly Richard is here. The excitement of seeing him never fades. The top is up on the Cadillac as he opens the door for me to climb in.

And then I catch the fragrance. I check the magnolia trees lining Alta. No blossoms. Too early yet. Jasmine?

Across the street, the hedge surrounding Bill Holden's building is not in bloom. Where is the aroma coming from? So unusual. Nothing I know. So penetratingly fragrant. I roll down the window to see if it is coming from outside. No. It is definitely inside the car. Our eyes meet as we simultaneously turn to look in the back seat. We both know, God is sitting in our back seat. We have no idea why God chooses to ride in the back seat of our Cadillac that night, but we feel an overwhelming sense of awe and wonderment. We don't speak but tears of joy stream down our faces as Richard starts the car.

We drive slowly over to Beverly Hills, out San Vicente, across Brentwood to Wilshire Boulevard. We continue up to Sunset to Miller Drive, winding our way toward Tom's home. Quietly we leave the car arm-in-arm, still in awe. The fragrance is still with us, and with it the incredible joy and mystery of being in the presence of God. The fragrance stops at Tom's doorstep.

I had thrilled to Richard's music in *State Fair*, *The Shocking Miss Pilgrim*, and Billy Rose's *Diamond Horseshoe*, the two latter films with Betty Grable. Maybe this movie will be the one with Maureen O'Hara and Harry James, which I haven't seen. It is still hard for me to believe that I am sitting at the feet of the man who made those films, his hand touching mine. We see the one with Maureen and Harry, *Do You Love Me?* In the last scene Betty Grable appears in a taxi waiting for Harry. Stories were simple then, boy meets girl, betrayal, misunderstandings, and reunion in brilliant technicolor.

At 1:00 AM, leaving Tom's house with several friends, one of the women remarks, "What is that delicious scent? It's much too early in the year for jasmine."

Richard and I say nothing. We stroll, holding hands, down the hill to his brown Cadillac. In months to come, the memory of the fragrance will sustain me. For now it eases the anxiety I have of living together without benefit of a marriage certificate.

When separating from my husband I left the Catholic Church. No more hypocrisy for me. Mostly it was because of "the pill."

In Mexico I had volunteered to help at the *Hospital de la Mujer*, The Woman's Hospital. This nearly 500 year old hospital had been built by Cortez. Rats ran rampant. Dead babies were targets. Nothing could be left outside of a refrigerator. The doctors trained us to deliver babies and instrument operations. Babies dropped out of women standing in line while they waited for a cot! We never had enough beds. The feet of one woman would be in the face of another.

A patient tugged on my arm. *"Senora, dime usted, sabe ?Que puedo hacer para no tener mas hijos?"* "Ma'am, tell me, do you know what I can do to stop having more children?"

Yes, I did know. I switched my volunteer service to an underground birth control clinic and joined the Unitarian Church. I missed the mysticism of Catholicism, but the fellowship and sincerity among Unitarians was refreshing. They did not throw Bible verses at each other. They knew each other personally, and they cared.

I was not certain who or what God was. I did know His attributes from my experience with the beautiful woman who had appeared in my living room in Westwood Village.

I was sitting on a sofa in my living room in Mexico City. An unseen hand pushed hard on my right shoulder. I fell on my knees as a male voice boomed through my body.

"God help me, in the name of Jesus Christ!"

I was amazed. *What is happening to me?* I thought of Barbara Roesch, my youngest daughter, Alexandra's, group leader at the Lutheran Church. Barbara's husband was in charge of the U.S. Trade Center in Mexico. Barbara, who had four children of her own, had allowed my daughter to stay at her home. Alexandra missed her brother and sister, who were at school in the States. The Roesch children gave Alex the family she needed. Barbara had told me of her own spiritual experiences. I wanted to share my experience with someone who would give me insight so I drove to her house.

But something was blocking my way, keeping me from arriving. *Tecamachalco* was a maddening network of circular streets near the *Lomas* where I lived. I do not know how I found her house. When I finally arrived, I felt I had been guided by an unseen source through a maze.

Unbeknownst to me, Barbara and her friends at the Lutheran church had been praying for me. She called on

Mr. Myer, the father of one of Alex' friends, to come over and pray with us. Mr. Myer came with his wife, another ordained minister from Tacoma, Washington, and his wife. Mr. Myer, a self ordained minister, bestowed on me the baptism of the Holy Spirit.

I began speaking in tongues.

I had been in a state of despair. My job had terminated as Assistant to the Director of USIU (U.S. International University's Mexico Campus). My closest friends were leaving for the States as the economy worsened. The man I thought I would marry went bankrupt and fled.

However, if you had asked me, I would have said, "I'm fine."

And worse yet, I would have believed it!

For five days we prayed together.

"Go to the City of Angels and be with the Jews," was the message I received.

Within five days I was flying to LAX (Los Angeles International Airport) ostensibly to attend my older daughter's graduation from Scripps in Claremont, California. In Los Angeles I met the Jewish doctors who became my trainers and teachers in clinical psychology.

Not wanting to join a church, I attended The Vineyard. Ken, the young minister, strummed his guitar and sang. Waves of love radiated from his caring soul. This had the effect of catching up young people in his web of non-intrusive missionary zeal.

I attended prayer meetings at Gaby Ferrer's guest house behind his mother's home. His mother, Rosemary Clooney, never joined us, but I would see her in the kitchen and remembered her hit song, "Come On-A My House." Prophetic!

The Vineyard owned nothing. They established a church in the sense of the first Christians who were called "the enlightened ones," for the simple reason that people could see halos shining around them. The early Christians met, as did the people of The Vineyard, in each other's homes. There was no membership. The Vineyard became the only Christ-directed fellowship I had among my atheist colleagues.

Those evenings in Gaby Ferrer's loft were special. He, too, had an unobtrusive, off-hand manner in leading this group of all ages. He could not have been more than nineteen, as was his girlfriend, singer Debbie Boone, who sometimes joined us.

On Sunday afternoons, The Vineyard borrowed Saint Paul's Methodist church in the San Fernando Valley for their musical praise and prayer service. Over a thousand followers would come together in song, sounding like a thousand angels.

Because of my marital situation, since meeting Richard, I have not been to The Vineyard. I miss their spirit.

Chapter 13

Richard balks, just as he does when I pull out the gilded, white, leather bound Bible that he prominently displays on his bookshelves, but refuses to touch. Just as he balks when I pray in the morning with a young man from the Findhorn Community in Scotland, who spent the night on our couch. Richard will not join in.

"God has told me to take you to the Vineyard," I insist. I can't imagine why I say that.

Richard promises to go the next Sunday. But when Sunday comes he conveniently has his children, Sean and Samantha, come to visit. God speaks to me again. The following Sunday, much unlike me, I announce with great authority, "You are coming to church."

Lo! and behold, he goes. At the beginning of each service at The Vineyard, people group together. Six or eight, will hold hands, pray silently or say whatever the spirit moves them to say. Like a lamb, Richard joins in. He holds my hand and that of the young lady next to him. When Ken finishes leading the songs of praise, then asks for those who wanted Christ to come into their life to raise their hands. Richard's hand rises. An hour and a half later, when Ken asks those who have raised their hands to come forward to the altar to receive the baptism of the Holy Spirit, he goes. I sit there, astonished. Never have I expected Richard to participate.

But once away from the service, driving back to Westwood, Richard lets go of a barrage of abuse and criticism.

"The music was terrible, too long," he says. "I thought they'd never end. The only thing that holds it together is Ken's love."

My high hopes are dashed. But God stops bugging me. I never bring up the matter again. I do not need to. Life does it for me. The honeymoon is over.

Richard sits me down, just before our move to the Marina.

"I have to tell you. There is no sign of any job. I haven't been paid for the last one. No money is coming in. I've sent Wendy something every month, but there isn't anything left to send. I'm a month behind on the rent. We can't go on."

"Can't you borrow from someone?"

"My credit's no good. I've been bankrupt twice."

"Your brother?"

I know his brother, Bob, who lives in Florida, is married to a DuPont heiress. I also know how Bob had resented the help Richard tried to give him on the Christmas that Bob had returned from the service. Richard was surprised by his brother's anger when Santa Claus Haymes arrived with a car loaded with presents for Bob's family.

"I don't want to, but I will. I have no choice."

He picks up the phone and dials Florida. Bob answers. Richard hedges around the subject. He cannot bring himself to ask outright. Maybe Bob can't grasp that his older brother desperately needs help. Older brothers are never supposed to need, they are the protectors and towers of strength. Richard never asks Bob for the help he needs.

"How much do you need?" I ask.

"Ten thousand. I need to move from here. Fifteen hundred a month is too much."

The rent is high for those days. My beautiful two bedroom, two bathroom apartment is only $400. But he doesn't want to share my place.

"I need a new hair piece, too," he adds. "Most of all, I need to take care of the abscesses in my mouth. It's the fault of the studio. They made all of us who were stars cap our teeth. My dentist says I need to clear them up as soon as possible."

I'm surprised. He has never complained. He has never spoken about his physical problems.

Abscesses, I think. *Oh, God, he can die from them!*

I call my broker in Cleveland. I borrow $10,000 on my stock. Parting with my financial cushion is not easy for the Depression baby I am. Money is not a subject I can even approach. My anxiety levels can cause me blackouts when confronted with the lack of it. My parents had fought and threatened divorce over it. My sister and I would huddle together, shaking in fear on our double bed during these episodes.

Despite my fear, I take the elevator to the basement garage, back my car out, and drive carefully up the ramp to Wilshire to avoid pedestrians. My mind is made up. As I pull onto Wilshire a car whizzes by, "Gutsy L" printed on the license plates. That affirms my intent. License plates in California have a knack for sending us messages from "upstairs." Ask anyone in L.A. When things go wrong, it is blamed on the full moon. In Mexico City, it is blamed on the altitude.

A bank draft made out to Richard Benjamin Haymes is in my hand the next morning. I give it to Richard.

"I can't take it. It could ruin our relationship."

I should have asked him how.

"God told me to give it to you," I lied.

Maybe He did, I think. *Heaven knows. There is no other way to make him take it. He has a deep seated reverence for God.*

He puts his arms around me. Holds me close. And sobs.

We move to Marina del Rey, the last place I would have chosen. The plastic, hotel atmosphere is comfortable for him. Not for me. I miss the fresh breezes from the cliffs of Santa Monica, the Birds of Paradise at my doorstep, the jungle of trees and plants I live in.

The Marina is barren. Cement and sailboats. Unhealthy vibrations come from the swingers and drug users. *This is the first stop after divorce*, I think.

The abscess problem explains Richard's loss of weight. His debility has reminded me too much of the cancer patients I had cared for in Mexico. But convincing Richard to make an appointment with his dentist is another matter.

Saying, "God is telling me to take you to the dentist," would be redundant.

So I make an appointment for myself. I arrange for Richard to pick me up. Without a word, his dentist plots with me. When Richard arrives the dentist impresses on Richard the urgency of the problem.

"Sure," Richard says, backing away. "I'll call you next week."

"The doctor says, 'now,' Richard," I reiterate as my voice begins escalating.

"Don't yell at me. Control yourself. You always have to make a scene in public."

"She's right, Richard," the dentist says. "She knows how dangerous it is. She's not making a scene. She loves you."

Richard and I are both shocked. I had never said it. I'm as afraid to speak of love as I am to speak of financial matters. Love was not expressed to us as children. We were not hugged or kissed.

The doctor leads Richard to the dental chair without further resistance.

"I can't give you an anesthetic. It's too late for that. It would be too dangerous if the abscess burst...In another twenty-four hours..."

In my mind, I finish his statement, *Another 24 hours and you would be dead!*

The teeth come out. Temporary plates go in. No sound from Richard. He never expresses pain. Not even in the months to come when his pain becomes far worse than the extractions. Surrender. If you do not, life will force you to. I know it, but I do not have the strength or the wisdom to make Richard understand...

Chapter 14

Testing: One, two, three. Testing: One, two three.

"Richie, what's the matter? Have I said something to offend you?"

"No!" he growled, "you haven't."

"Would you like me to leave?" I am running through the gamut of psychological interventions.

"No!" More vehemently. "I don't want you to leave."

"You must be hurting badly to be so angry." I have saved this for the last.

He stops. At least temporarily. The next day when I return from my office, he begins again, finding fault. He topped off his tirade, "And don't tell me I'm hurting."

I can think of nothing to say. My clinical repertoire is exhausted. Should I leave? Should I put up with this verbal abuse as I had for sixteen years with my husband? What am I feeling as I look at him, so angry and bitter? I...feel love. Tears well up in my eyes. "It doesn't seem to matter what you do, I never stop loving you."

He walks away from me. In a few minutes he's back.

"That's how I feel about you."

With those words, we are married, as much as a couple who exchanged vows on an altar.

He is drinking, of course, only I don't realize it at first. Alone all day, too proud to go out with people he knows while he is jobless, he frequents the myriad bars around the Oakwood Apartments (a Mexican place in particular) rather than finish his script or autobiography. He leaves me a note:

"Meet me over at Casa Escobar."

I find him in conversation with whatever stranger has recognized him. The managers and bartenders are delighted and make him feel welcome. I can tell how much Vodka he consumes by the extent of his anger and the loss of his appetite. His dinner is returned to the kitchen, untouched.

Little things have changed.

"You can open your own car door. We don't need to put on that act anymore."

Again, I say nothing. I hadn't known it was an act.

Testing...testing.

I insist he see a specialist. The fear of cancer is unspoken, but there. He has gained some weight and is looking younger, no longer frail since the bout with the dentist. I want to be certain. I confront fear. He agrees to be tested.

As we leave Dr. Matsumoto's office after the final examination, I am trembling and disoriented, uncertain where I am—two blocks west of Camden Drive, where I go every day to my office. The street seems to rise up and meet my feet. I have to take Richard's arm to keep from falling. I cannot confront the thought of losing him.

God, let me have five years, I beg silently.

At least five years. My father died at sixty-five. Richard will be sixty-one in September.

Oh, God. Pull him through, I pray.

Richard asks me to regress him one more time. He goes all the way back to his birth. No conversation. Just some gurgling sounds, tears, choking, smothered mumblings.

"I am at my mother's breast," he says. "There is too much milk. I am drowning in it."

Richard's first experience with his mother after birth was life-threatening. The fear of intimacy and the fear of death are synonymous for him. No wonder he kept changing wives.

One of our rituals is a weekly visit to Woodland Hills to see Dan Amick, a chiropractor, one of my colleagues in bioenergetics training. Dan and I are experimenting with the connection between muscular manipulation, emotional release, and characterological change. The manipulation is relaxing, so Richard has a treatment too.

As we are walking through the open air parking lot this balmy June day after our treatments, Richard suddenly tightens his grip on me and swings me around to face him. Fear sweeps over me. He cannot have been drinking. He was with me all morning. Richard holds me tightly.

"I want you to know how much I love you," he says, intensely. "How much I appreciate what you have done for me. I owe you my life. No one has ever loved me as you have. No one on this earth, among all the people I know, would have done for me what you have done. You have given me everything you had.

He releases his grasp. "Music was my mistress and my life. It was my constant companion. It inspired me and kept me going. Music is no longer my mistress." He pauses. "You are."

I am so overwhelmed that I can't hear the words bursting out of him into my deafened ears on that warm sunny day, the breeze rustling through the Eucalyptus trees. I can't respond. I am choking on my emotions.

Later, I ask him to write down the words he has spoken. He never does, until after his...

Dr. Matsumoto calls on the Fourth of July. "No cancer. I wanted you to know as soon as possible. Not a trace."

The good doctor had gone to work on a holiday to ease our anxiety. How we celebrate that day! The joy of being free from fear. So many of both his friends and mine have succumbed to cancer.

He begins to eat the food he orders. He respects the care I take of myself, and drinks Arrowhead Spring water and takes vitamins with me. The boyish cut of his new hairpiece and the few added pounds remove fifteen years from his handsome face. He begins to take walks with me. I jog in the morning. Returning from dinner that night, we skip down Admiralty Way in a fine drizzle, arm-in-arm like ice skaters, singing, "Skipping in the rain."

His agent calls. "How would you like to open in Philadelphia next month? Yeah, *The Big Broadcast of 1944* with Harry James...No, it's a show. They're planning to take it to Broadway."

We sit cuddled up on the sofa listening one more time to the songs from his album *As Time Goes By*.
"Life was so new, so very bright,
Ages ago, last night ... "
We have been given another chance.
God is good.

"This above all remember, study 8-18 of Isaiah."

Chapter 15

"Are you sure you want to come? When I'm working I'm awful to be around."

Richard's words of warning cannot diminish my excitement. Everything is going well. Richard looks terrific. Life is joy again. He has stopped drinking in deference to the show. He is working out, getting his body in shape to resonate those long drawn out baritone notes that carry a listener to the infinite and beyond.

I come running into the bedroom, bounce on the bed, check book in hand.

"I've made it," I scream in delight. "I've made it!"

On my own in my own business, I have earned two thousand dollars in one month. It is enough to live on. I will not have to work for someone else. I can do what I like and stay alive while doing it. I feel I can afford to be away for ten days. Nothing is going to stop me from being with Richard opening night. I want to be immersed in his world of show business. I want to know him and understand him.

Richard is taking an interest in my life, also. He has accompanied me to celebrate the June Equinox in Topanga Canyon with my more far out friends. He is critical, but precise in his evaluations of people. He dispenses with the unreal, the phony. His politics, his thinking, if not always his behavior, are conservative. I avoid discussing Ronald Reagan.

Richard suffers shame and guilt for what he considers having not measured up to his own standards, but he suffers silently. His numerous marriages and his separation from his six children are painful subjects. He speaks of buying a house in the Santa Monica Canyon near my apartment where we can live with two of his children.

He begins taking an interest in my practice, especially in one of my patients, Sara, a young actress who had been raped. She needs advice.

"Should I drop the legal action against this rapist," she questions on the phone. "Won't the PR man for my soap be furious with me. You know, the publicity of a court trial..." She pauses. "I don't want that SOB to get away with it. And I don't want to lose my job. I've struggled so long to get on the show."

Overhearing, Richard takes the phone from me. "Actually, this will be an opportunity for you to get good press coverage. YOUNG STAR FIGHTS BACK. Great headlines! It could make an episode on your soap." He has a knack for turning a negative into a positive.

Forty years in show business, I think while he is speaking.

Richard tolerates my Findhorn friends. During a visit with Peter Caddy, the founder of the Findhorn Community in Scotland, he listens politely to our conversation. But when it no longer interests him, he quietly removes himself to the other end of the living room and listens to his music.

We continue our conversation, though our guest seems uneasy. Recalling his days in Encino with Joanne Dru, I too feel uncomfortable. In his mind, not only is his action not offensive, but he is doing us a favor. This is his way of saying, "Enjoy yourselves, you don't need me." It would never occur to Richard that his behavior could be misconstrued as rude.

A friend has invited me to be on his talk show *Science Safari.* The subject, of course, is psychology.

Sunny Lash, my confidante, accompanies us to my television debut. Sunny had been the personal assistant to Laurence Olivier and Vivian Leigh during their difficult years in Hollywood while they were both married to someone else. Like Richard and me. In those years Hollywood had a false veneer of propriety and was skittish about any hint of scandal.

Sunny and Richard sit together while I am taping the show. Sunny buried two husbands, both in show business. Her last husband was a well known director. She and Richard know many of the same people.

Later I learn from Sunny what they talked about.
"I'm so proud of her," Richard says.

"She can do anything she really wants to. She handles people with such a professional manner," Sunny agrees.

"That's the way she handles me." He grins. "I have to keep myself aware of the fact that I am being manipulated most of the time."

"Yes, you do. You'll have to watch out or she'll be in control and you won't know what the hell is going on. You won't know what day of the week it is."

"He adores you, but he's lost without you," Sunny whispers to me, before she leaves us.

How strange her words seem to me. I feel so dependent on him.

One night not long after we moved to the Oakwood Apartments, I have an unusual experience similar to those out-of-body states described in Dr. Karagulla's book, *Breakthrough to Creativity*. I tell Richard the next morning.

"I am sitting on the edge of my bed. I have been taken somewhere. My body is lying beside me. Beyond, I can see you asleep. It is dark, but a street light is shining through the window. Next to me, leaning against the wall stands a handsome, twenty-six year old spaceman, all in shades of blue from his belted tunic to his knee boots. I'm not into space stuff, nor *Star Wars*, so I feel weird."

This space cadet repeats indifferently, "This above all remember, study 8 through 18 of Isaiah. And when Rabbi Lerer is made Chief Rabbi of Jerusalem, you are to go to Israel."

Richard makes no comment. I reach for pen and paper and write down exactly what the spaceman said. Months go by before I can tell the story to Rabbi Lerer in Mexico City.

We arrive at the Philadelphia airport for *The Big Broadcast*, and are taken to a theater in the round in Valley Forge. That evening rehearsals begin. *The Big Broadcast of 1944* opens the next day. Richard exchanges a few magic words with Harry James, followed by a run through with an ever-changing script, and then the final rehearsal. Richard closes the show. I am amazed. The rehearsal lasts three hours. I recall the weeks we spent before opening night on our musicals for the Junior League in Mexico City.

Helen Forrest, Don Wilson and Hildegard from the east (all of them) are a delight. But Harry James most of all!

The theater is new. The dressing rooms are suites. The two male stars are together again. Harry promptly sets up bar. He finds out what I like to drink, vodka tonic, and every evening he prepares it for me, in anticipation of my arrival.

The next day the publicists take us to Philadelphia for radio and television interviews. Richard wants me to accompany him. I am ignored, but at the same time treated politely. Someone bustles about to find a seat for me. The usual trite questions are asked but with sincerity and interest. The people of Philadelphia live up to their reputation as "The City Of Brotherly Love."

Richard wants me in the audience for his television appearance so that I can observe him and watch the monitor also. I put on my therapist shingle and analyze.

"How was I?"

"You were breezy, carefree, and really good looking."

He complains about the repetitious questions but he is pleased. His answers are just as repetitious, such as where are you living? What are you doing now? But this is what the audience wants, so everyone says. This is the image forty years of singing, scandal, and movie making have created. From boy-next-door to devil-may-care, to laid-back, to Hollywood has-been. No, not has-been, drop-out is a better word. He has never stopped working, even though he was in Europe for fifteen years, singing. Oddly, the public does not remember his incredible voice, but rather the number of his wives, bankruptcies, and alcoholic episodes—in that order.

His television appearances pay off. By 8:30 PM, curtain time, every one of the three thousand seats are sold. Lee Guber, the producer, is elated. He invites us to a special dinner after the show. Richard and Don Wilson are the only cast members invited. Lee Guber is a businessman, a successful one. The other guests must have been backers, invited to be impressed. Lee owns the theater. He owns the show.

Don Wilson sits on my left. He shares with me something of his life as an announcer/comedian for Jack Benny, both in radio and on television. A bond builds between us that helps me through the long hours of waiting. Show business is a waiting business; then hurry up and run. Don is very kind to me when *The Big Broadcast of 1944* comes to Los Angeles the following year.

Without Dick Haymes.

Chapter 16

As Richard runs onto the stage from mid-aisle after a rousing intro from Harry James and the boys, I ease my way to the back of the last row of seats, leaning on the wall as I watch him close the show. He sings the popular songs from *State Fair* that everyone remembers.

"I'm as breathless as a willow in a windstorm... "

I reminisce. I am twelve in Rocky River, Ohio, population ten thousand. I am leaning against the tall ash tree in my front yard. I am singing:

**"Oh, I haven't seen a crocus or a rosebud,
Or a robin on the wing ...**

Can this be true? I ask myself, now back in the present. I am standing here, the person closest in heart to this marvelous man that three thousand people have come to see. *Can this be me?*

He tells the audience about making *State Fair,* about the wonderful, endearing actors including Blue Boy the prize pig. There is laughter and smiles as they remember, too. After a romantic song from the war years, the entire cast joins him one by one, singing "This Is the Army, Mr. Green." He asks the audience to join in "God Bless America." The tears stream down my face. I have come home at last.

Richard is first off stage to a thunderous applause. I move to the exit where I can greet him, give him a big hug, and walk off with him arm-in-arm. I go to his dressing room amidst fans pressing him for his autograph. With his clothes half off, lines of people march through his dressing room for his signature. I sit at his side, amazed at the clamor for a view of him in his T-shirt.

"Darling, don't you want to put on a shirt?"

"What for?"

"You're in your underwear in front of all these people."

"So what?"

Fastidious Mr. Haymes greets his fans in his underwear. But, he wants me right there. It is not until days later that I realize people did notice me.

On Saturday there is a matinee. I choose that time to leave. Richard is at his worst in the first hours after waking, which is at 1:00 or 2:00 o'clock in the afternoon, so I go jogging to stay out of his way.

"Where are you going?" he'd invariably yell, as if I am abandoning him.

"I'm going jogging, but I'll stay if you want me to." I know he doesn't want me there, but he needs to tell me to go.

"You have to leave," he answers. "You know I can't stand having anyone around when I'm doing Yoga and vocalizing."

Fortunately the Hilton, where we are staying is out in the countryside of Valley Forge. I find a great place for running to ease the strain I am beginning to feel.

After the show, we go out, sometimes with other cast members. The two comedians are great fun. I wish I could remember their names.

But when we are alone, he begins the fault finding. He is not drinking. (In those days I don't know that sobriety does not make a person sober.) He starts the negativity at breakfast.

"Wouldn't you like to eat something?" I see the table full of food the hotel waiter brought, now turning cold.

"I'm not hungry," he snaps.

"Would you like to eat with me later?"

"No!" he barks. "You know I don't eat before a show!"

The words themselves are not harsh, it is his tone of voice that makes me shrivel and leave.

Then he does his Yoga and vocalizing, eats an early dinner and goes to the theater by himself. I go with some of the cast members, sometimes by myself. Once at the theater, he is "on" again. Behind stage he and Harry can reminisce for hours about their days together traveling through the U.S. on a bus with the band.

"Remember the time when we were so broke we couldn't eat?" laughs Harry. "We—"

"—picked up that hooker," Haymes chimes in.

"And she bought us dinner and gave us a place to

sleep." Harry laughs harder.

"And she didn't even get laid!" Haymes cackles.

Life on the road moving from town to town in a bus with the boys in the band is painful, lonesome, anxiety ridden drudgery. Their shared trials bring them together like brothers. The worse the trials the more they laugh.

Years later when both have climbed to the height of their stardom and then fallen, Harry calls to be rescued. He needs Richard to return to the band. Richard breaks a signed contract to open on Broadway in *Pal Joey* in order to help his pal Harry. That show would have saved Richard's floundering career. The part made Gene Kelly a star.

At night, leaving the stage door together, I catch a glimpse of the adoration that women have for film idols. They stand there waiting to touch him, see him, to fan the flames of their fantasies. "Fan" is a great name for them, though the origin is surely from the word "fanatic." They like to talk to me also when they realize who I am. They ask me if we are married.

"No, no," I respond. "We just live together."

My Puritanical mind notes that this in no way diminishes my stature with them, with the exception of one fan, Anna Poole. Anna is the head of the Dick Haymes Fan Club. But more than that, she is a member of the family, ready to help any one of his children or him, at a moment's notice. Although she's married, Anna is obviously enraptured with Richard. This kind of behavior from women makes Richard particularly distant. With a stranger, he can enjoy the sexual overtones, but not from someone like Anna. He would often have me take her phone calls.

"It's Anna," I'd call out.

"You take it."

"He's in the shower," I lie. "He'll be glad to hear you've called."

In one of my vulnerable moments when Richard has reduced me to tears I make the mistake of going to Anna's room for emotional support. I look at her as a mother figure.

Anna's response to my dilemma is exactly the same as my Spanish mother-in-law. *"Hay que aguantar,* you will have to stand it. You'll have to get used to it if you're going to stay with him," she admonishes sharply. "What do you expect? You're going around with a celebrity!" As if being a celebrity is a justifiable excuse for outrageous behavior.

From the shrill tone of voice, I know she really is saying, "You fool! Appreciate the fact that you have the most desirable man in this world in bed with you. What I wouldn't give to be there in your place, you idiot!"

Men have always sought me out. At ten I was dating. I do not understand this starvation for male affection.

That night I am standing in the dark, leaning against the wall at the back of the theater listening to Richard sing those love songs that penetrate the heart of every woman who has come to hear him. I am approached out of the darkness by a woman from the audience.

"Are you his wife?" she whispers.

I am startled. This woman could have been me. She is

attractive, well-dressed, the kind of woman who is easily accepted into the Junior League.

"No, I'm not. We live together," I stammer.

"What is it like when he makes love to you?"

I am jarred by the question. Nothing is private anymore. How can she ask me this? I am unable to answer her. I mumble some inaudible truism and look away.

Chapter 17

Besides the books I have mentioned, Richard and I read and discuss a document of great interest to me. He introduced it to me in the second volume of a set which the U.S. Government had published for the bicentennial. The document is called "The Prophecy of George Washington."

One night in 1777, General Washington gave orders not to be disturbed. He was in his tent at Valley Forge when a beautiful woman suddenly appeared before him. She showed him the future of our nation, saying, "Son of the Republic; look and learn."

She rolled back a mist through which he could see the three crises that will befall the growing country as it extends from shore to shore: the Indian wars the settlers face; brother fighting brother to preserve the Union; and the final crisis when, "All the world shall not prevail against her." She will be attacked on both shores, every city and town will be reduced to rubble, and the few remaining Americans left to fight "were nigh well overcome" with defeat and despair. When an army of angels descended and inspired them to keep fighting until they pushed the enemy into the sea. "And this nation shall remain on earth as long as the dew falls from the heavens."

I decide to see Valley Forge for myself. The words the beautiful woman had spoken to George Washington ring through my ears as I wander over the green hills, map in hand. One of the guards helps me pick out the place where George Washington's tent had been in 1777. A large tree spreads its limbs over the spot.

I sit down under that tree and think about the mystery of life. A fluke has brought me and Richard together. A few words in a Yoga book. A few words from someone "upstairs" who directed me to The City of Angels. Is it someone "upstairs" who blanked out my mind that day in Santa Monica, so that I missed an appointment with a new patient and met Richard instead. I always felt my patients came from God. Maybe Richard did too.

As I sit there, I try to relive the scene between General Washington and the beautiful woman. Was she the same incredibly beautiful lady I had encountered in my living room that August day in Westwood Village, who had allowed me to cross over into the other world? Was I, too, chosen to do something special? All God had said was go to Israel when Rabbi Lerer is made Chief Rabbi. Not very spectacular. Not like building a nation. Why is God talking to me and telling me what to do? Why is my pathway being guided and prepared for me? Why do I apparently have so much? Why do others, like that poor woman who found me in the darkness of a summer theater audience among three thousand people, need to ask me, "What is it like when he makes love to you?"

Oh, God, I think, *is there so little love on this earth that...*

The tears stinging my eyes are for the lonely lives of all my sisters yearning for love and passion. And yet this incredible love I enjoy with Richard, even in the greatest moments we have, cannot be compared to the love I have experienced in our parallel universe. Sexual expression is an anachronism in that world. Love in that world is beyond comparison.

Oh, if I could only share that experience in the Light with every man, woman and child, I think, *we would have a different world overnight.*

"Oh, God. Oh, God," I pray softly, "Why don't you show yourself to all of them? Why me? Why Me? I don't even follow your written commandments. You have guided my footsteps to my Jewish teachers. You found me the money for my training. You found me patients to treat and guided me in their treatment. You kept me functioning through those hours of State Board Exams when my left brain ceased to function because of thirty days of horrendous electroshock treatments and rape. You kept me on course when my soul was in despair, walking on the edge of madness. Oh, God, why am I so special to you?

"Why?"

"Where have you been?" The musicians ask me that night at the theater. "You missed this afternoon's performance."

They surprise me. I am not aware that I had become

conspicuous by my absence.

Helen Forrest, one of the great female vocalist of the 40's, has helped me order a birthday cake for Richard. It is his sixty-first birthday. The plan is for Harry James to stop the show as I come down the aisle with this enormous cake, all sixty-one candles burning. I was shaking all over. I know how particular Richard is about his performance so I am afraid to do anything so unusual. I am so afraid of his anger.

"Do you think it will upset him?" I ask the drummer.

"If you can't give him a surprise birthday cake, you don't have any relationship anyway," the drummer assures me.

I am determined. I stand midway down the aisle to the stage, waiting for Harry's signal, trembling so much I fear the candles will go out. As Harry speaks, I begin my slow march to the stage to the beat of "Happy Birthday to You."

My wedding song.

I hold the enormous cake as I greet Richard, my eyes blinking in the bright spotlight. "Happy Birthday, Darling. I love you."

In front of 3,000 unknown witnesses he responds, "I love you, too." I hand him the cake and we are married.

Do not ask me what I wore to my wedding. I can't remember. I only remember from that moment on, I am his wife.

Chapter 18

"That is the first birthday cake I have ever received." Richard is not angry.

Six wives and a mother, and no birthday cake? How sad. But I am amazed and pleased that I was the first to give him one. I like feeling special.

A friend of mine from Philadelphia joins us at a luncheon honoring Richard. The press has issued the invitation. We throw our arms around each other. For me it is stabilizing to reunite with someone from my past. I have become so absorbed in Richard's life, I am off balance. I notice Richard watching us from the head table as we embrace and exchange confidences from the past five years.

Envy is not the word for the expression on Richard's face. It is more like wistfulness, a kind of longing, of being left out. He certainly has friends. He and Harry James have been laughing and sharing stories by the hour. I am going to see that same expression again, when we meet my son, Javier, at Los Angeles International Airport later in the month.

Hildegard, the amusing pianist in the cast, gives me

the warmest goodbye. We have become friendly driving back and forth to the theater. She has even complimented me on my singing when we all burst into song on the way home—home being the Hilton Hotel. She knows I will be leaving the company before the opening on Long Island. The rest of the company assume I am a permanent fixture. A private practice back in Los Angeles is no excuse for leaving the show.

A limousine is sent for us to traverse from Valley Forge across new Jersey to New York City for another press conference. This time we will be at the Press Club opposite the Rainbow Room on the top floor of Radio City. This interview is not just to push the *Big Broadcast of 1944*, which is moving to another theater-in-the-round on Long Island, but to begin a campaign to revive the Rainbow Room with music and stars from the 40's. Richard is scheduled to sing there after closing in Detroit at the end of October, to be followed with an interview on national television for *The Dick Cavett Show*. I am thrilled. Everything is happening for us, God is still good!

The Press Club, on the top floor of Rockefeller Center, is jammed. Television cameras, radio announcers, photographers, everyone talks at once.

"This is the largest gathering of the press in New York City in twenty years," I hear the excited radio announcer say as Richard and I are pushed through the crowd.

Richard holds my arm tightly as long as he can. But the crush becomes too great. He is pushed toward the microphones and television cameras. I emerge on the fringe of the circle of men and women yelling, shouting out questions, scribbling his answers.

After ten minutes of the usual questions and Richard's glib answers, a reporter, pointing at me, shouts over the noise from the milieu. "Who's she?"

In the split second of silence that the crowd's attention shifts to me, Richard breaks through the mob, grabs my arm, whisks me into an elevator before I can answer. The interview is over.

Standing on the street corner waiting for our limousine, we run into Johnny Desmond and Fran Warren. It is true. Stand on a street corner in New York City and you will eventually run into everyone you know. For Richard, it took less than a minute. He knows so many people, and yet a strange quality is surfacing. Aloneness.

I remember the days when I would go to my office. Supposedly he is working on his autobiography or the script for *Reprise*. He never complains about being alone. He never complains.

The chauffeur entertains us with Mafia stories as he drives us to a new hotel on Long Island. He has worked for people highly connected to that world. He retired alive, and enjoys driving.

Richard is a great listener when it comes to chauffeurs, maids, valets and waitresses. Wherever we go, he immediately befriends them and soon knows their history. I am much less democratic.

Our room at the hotel is black and red. I accept Richard's apology for our dismal accommodations. I realize I have made a mistake. The room is small, airless, viewless. Richard reads me too well for me to pretend. He sees the disapproval on my face when I come through the door.

"You don't like it, do you?" he snaps.

"It's not my idea of décor," I answer blandly.

"There's nothing I can do about it. It's the only hotel near the theater."

"Richie, it's okay. I'll be leaving tomorrow. It's only for one night. At least we're together."

Nothing I can say moves him from the anger and bitterness that descends upon me. It isn't what he says; it is the sneering, derogatory way he says it. I lay there quietly, wanting to make love. I will not fight with him, perhaps out of fear. I simply withdraw into myself, saying nothing; not defending, not blaming. I simply vanish.

In the morning the barrage of expletives continues. I eat breakfast in stony silence. While I pack my bags, the haranguing is ceaseless.

"I should never have brought you here. I should never have let you come. I knew this would happen."

I finish packing, slam the lid shut, call for the bellhop and a taxi. There are no goodbyes. I leave for the airport, La Guardia or Kennedy. I don't remember.

Once the plane is airborne, I unfasten my seat belt, I lock myself in the bathroom and for most of the next five hours flight back to Los Angeles, I pound the walls and scream. Ten days of frustration, of highs and lows, unbridled rage pour out of me. Whether I go to my place in Santa Monica, or to our place in the Marina, I do not know. All I know is that by 9:00 PM he reaches me by phone. Wherever I am, he acts as if nothing is wrong.

"Darling, how are you?"

"Richie, I'm fine," I say while I seethe inside.

"The show's a sell-out again. A smashing success. They love it."

"I'm so glad."

"Everyone asks for you and sends their love."

"I send my love, too."

"I miss you."

"I miss you, too," I answer as I begin to thaw.

He calls me every night until he comes back to the Marina where I wait for him.

I am overjoyed to see him.

When I married my Spanish husband, I thought I had married my Italian father. I soon discovered I had wed my English-American mother. There was no other way than mother's way. Nothing at all existed outside of her realm of consciousness. Her grudges were long lasting and required daily expression. My father, on the other hand, would yell, shout, then forget what the problem was all about. This time I found myself married to my father. I begin to acquire empathy for my mother.

My work keeps me in balance. Tom Cooper and I plan another surprise birthday party for Richard, with another birthday cake. He is surprised and pleased. He is persuaded to sing along with the rest of us in fun.

Oh, those were happy days, "When we were young, last night."

"Wendy wants me to take Sean," Richard says as he hangs up the phone. "I said I would have to talk with you."

For me, children always come first. I had stayed with a man I stopped loving for fourteen years to provide a proper home and security for my children. A boy needs to have a father, especially one just thirteen.

I say, "Yes."

The next time Richard has to leave for the show, Sean stays with family friends in Malibu. I take him my bicycle. We spend the day swimming, enjoying each other immensely. My son is in Alaska. How wonderful to have a son again.

Richard and I are still so happy. Everything, including Sean, is working out. No problem is insurmountable. God is on the side of lovers. Offers of work are pouring in. The lean days are over. Richard budgets carefully and goes over it with me.

He offers me ten percent of all his earnings off the top. But I do not want money. I want respectability. His female fans and cast members accept our situation but I feel a certain snideness from others. Perhaps I imagine it. But the, "Who is she?" annoys me once too often. I want to be his wife legally.

"Ten percent isn't what I want. A wife would have fifty percent."

"A wife would have one hundred percent." He sounds bitter.

In California, life is different. A woman is expected to support herself, although Richard's world is like mine. He pays all the bills, picks up all the checks. A man in Mexico would be highly insulted if a woman attempted to retrieve a check at a restaurant. Yet, Richard is proud of the way I am making it on my own. Nevertheless, as we drive by a shop on Rodeo Drive he is ashamed.

"I used to buy three hundred dollar handbags for Rita in that store," he says.

One day while shopping together in the Santa Monica Mall, we stop in to see a diamond merchant Richard met while having a watch repaired. I am speechless when he asks the merchant to show us some diamonds for earrings for me. I can tell he does not consider the matched pair I choose to be large enough. The jeweler designs the Tiffany setting.

"Diamonds are a Gift of Love," the sign above the showcase reads.

Richard nods. I erase the thought that he is buying them for me because he does not like the gold loops I usually wear. In the recesses of my mind, I see one diamond set in a ring.

Later he says, "My God, Dianne, why do you want to marry me? I'm a six time loser. If I marry you, I'll bust it."

I insist. "I will wait until January. You can make up your mind then. That will be one year of being together. I need to be married. I can't handle it when you introduce me as, 'This is my Lady.' I feel like you are saying 'This is my mistress.'"

I will live to regret those words.

The shadows are few. The days are bright and sunny in Los Angeles. I arrive at our Marina del Rey apartment at 7:00 in the evening. The candles are burning and he is waiting for me. Wendy leaves us alone now that we have Sean and she has monthly checks again.

"She'll find some way to wreck us," Richard warns me.

Then he leaves for Detroit.

Chapter 19

Richard

It has been six years since I sat with you and wrote those few pages, me here and you there. Javier, your son, is with me after his death on Oahu. He gets through to you better than I do by just talking. I need to set things up like the license plate ILUV487, or trigger you into pushing the right button on the radio to hear me sing to you.

How long ago I sang that song for you in Detroit. I was getting weaker and weaker. I was drinking to keep going. I didn't think I could make it through another show. You walked into the restaurant where I was eating with Fran Warren before going on Sunday night, the last night of *The Big Broadcast of 1944* in Detroit. I greeted you curtly, and kept on talking to Fran.

I was scared. I'd never felt that way before—so weak. The alcohol wasn't helping. When I took a drink I saw your look of disaproval. You didn't say anything, but you knew. You knew I never drink when I'm working. I didn't know what to say to you, so I kept talking to Fran. I was glad you'd come. I could never quite believe you could love me. What was I? An aging old man. The "Old Pelican." An alcoholic. I waited 'til close to my death to admit that to you.

You sat there so patiently, not saying too much. How could you? I deliberately prattled on with Fran about trifles. We discussed the set-up at the Rainbow Room, the sound, the audience. We were supposed to leave Detroit for New York the next day. I knew already I could not go and my fear was that you would leave me. Now I really needed you and was too afraid to tell you how much. I had never felt this weak before—even when I had TB. What was happening to me?

You had flown to Detroit to be with me for the closing night, then on to New York City for the Dick Cavett Show.

We went back to the hotel room.

"I can't go on to New York, I'm too sick," I blurted out. "You can go if you want, the ticket is here."

For a split second I could see you waiver—your disappointment, the plans you made trashed. You were looking forward to seeing Dr. Pierrakos, a psychiatrist you had trained with. You had a session lined up with him. I didn't tell you how incredibly sick I felt. Some sound in my voice, perhaps a sound of desperation, caught you, grabbed you and you turned. I saw the surge of anger, frustration, and disappointment leave your face. You looked at me as if for the first time, with alarm.

You said the right words. "Of course I won't go. I'll

stay with you. If you don't feel strong enough to go to L.A., we can go to my mother's house near Cleveland, in Rocky River."

You made it possible for me to go on that night. You knew and I knew, that your presence there in front of me, held my hand that gripped the microphone. Kept me from falling off the stage. Like an air current that lifts a spread-winged eagle, your presence lifted me. You had not abandoned me nor betrayed me. You were there for me, not for what I could give you. I knew I had nothing left to give anyone. But, for me ...

"The more I see you,
The more I want you.
Somehow this feeling
Just grows and grows."

I sang that song as if I were singing every word for the first time; as if I were seeing you for the first time. I felt the surge of that air current running between us, lifting me up and carrying me, steadying my hand.

"With every sigh I become
More mad about you,
More lost without you.
And so it goes,"

I was afraid to tell you how much I loved you, so afraid you would be overwhelmed and leave.

"Can you imagine?"

The fear was spiraling me downward again. The music caught me this time, the only friend I ever had until I met you.

"How much I love you."

On those words I started to rise again. Strength came back into my legs. I could lean less on the mike.

"As years go by,
You know the only one
For me can only be you.
My arms won't leave you,
My heart won't try."

I don't remember much about the rest of the show, except the end. It was our last night, our last show. I realized I would never sing again.

I stopped the show.

I wanted to take that moment to thank all the people that had made my life possible, my music possible. Music was my life. I turned to thank Harry and the boys. Without them behind me and you in front of me, I could not have made it. But most of all, darling, I thanked whatever God there was out there, for you.

You met me in the dressing room. I was seated in front of the mirror in my T-shirt removing makeup and looking old and frail. Lee Guber, the producer of the show, came in, bullying and berating.

"How unprofessional! This isn't a bandstand, it's a show. It's legitimate theater. Why in the hell did you have to stop and thank the audience? My God, Dick, how could you act like such an amateur?"

There was a wild look in your eyes—like "kill." If you had a gun, you would have wasted him. You were about to say something.

I looked up at you and ordered, "Don't!"

I could see you bite your lip. As soon as Lee was out

of the room, you let it out. "How could you let him stand there and—"

I cut you off. "It's simple. He pays me to do a show."

So, how did I thank you? Did I tell you what was in my heart? No. I complained. I found fault. I talked to the waitresses. I ignored you as I had the evening you arrived when I kept on talking to Fran while we ate.

We waited for the results from the Detroit doctor. He was evasive. I ordered food and then ignored it. I drank. You watched, waited and sat there. I wondered how much you could take. You tried to persuade me to go to Cleveland. I wouldn't budge. It was L.A. or nothing. New York was screaming. I had to cancel *The Dick Cavett Show*. Again, I saw the disappointment flood your face. What were you thinking? How are we going to live? No, you weren't. You were wracking your brain about my symptoms. The doctor ruled out cancer last July. So what could it be? Fever? Pneumonia? That's what you hit on. You had known someone once with sudden pneumonia that left them weak.

You sat in that hotel room in Detroit for three days, one of which was your birthday, while we waited for my strength to return. When American Airlines found us a non-stop, first class flight back to L.A., I was finally strong enough to get on it.

The night before we left, we strolled nearby the hotel. We entered a tall, majestic building in the ornate style they used to build. The central foyer was lit. It reached up endlessly to the sky like the atrium of a Roman house. You began to sing:

"Oh, beautiful, for spacious skies
For amber waves of grain.
For purple mountains majesty,
Above the fruited plain,"

It was the first time you sang alone to me since we first met. I had told you how it grated on my ears to hear you sing off key. You were not singing off key, you were right on, full, rich and beautiful.

"America, America,
God shed thy grace on thee.
And crown thy good with brotherhood,
From sea to shining sea."

I applauded. I realized that you weren't afraid of me anymore. Your eyes were shining like the sea. You were totally yourself with this God of yours that gave you strength from somewhere. You looked happy again.

American Airlines personnel greeted us warmly at the airport with a wheelchair. I gratefully accepted. I enjoyed the ride and the attention I was getting. Like old times. I was wheeled all the way to the plane.

"Dick Haymes, Dick Haymes," people whispered.

You enjoyed it too. Now that you had your God back, New York was forgotten. It didn't matter; wasn't to be. Never was to be.

First Class provided champagne. I accepted it in large quantities. I had eaten little in three days.

Testing ... testing ... one, two three.

You sat there, thick auburn hair falling on your blond mink coat. Your face fresh, eyes dancing.

So I had to kill it.

"When I get back to Los Angeles, I hope you'll understand, but I can't be with just one woman."

You let out a yell. I could feel you rise out of your seat. On one glass of champagne, you had no interest in the public around you.

What did you say? I don't remember. A howling pain is what I recall. The words don't matter, just the anger and the pain, and the yell. Then I twisted the knife.

"Do you always have to make a scene in public?"

Chapter 20

November 1979

Richard refuses to see a doctor. Back among the palm trees on familiar territory, he is his obstinate self. He goes as far as the chiropractor, who takes x-rays of his lungs.

"You must see a doctor immediately." Dan is kind enough to wait until after Thanksgiving Day to give us the warning.

Richard asks me to be a co-signer and co-partner with him in his new company. My friend and colleague, Leslie Waldo, recommended that I consider the tax liabilities. I know Richard owes money to the IRS, and anything to do with money frightens me. I remember my parent's battles and say no, in favor of his naming his eldest daughter Pidge. I encourage him in any way I can to renew and strengthen the ties with his family. If Nugent, her sister, comes over to see him, I find an excuse to leave so the two of them can be alone together. He is so ashamed and guilty about being an absentee father, I have to push him to call his own family.

I remember the look on his face when my son, Javier, and I embraced at the airport.

"Hang on to this one, Mom." Javier liked him.

If Richard speaks about dying I retort, "What makes you think I won't go first?"

With that, he insists I stop flying with the Flying Samaritans, a medical group I fly with to bring treatment to people in the remote mountainous area of Mexico. I am translator and psychotherapist.

Richard had stopped piloting a plane years before. He blacked out once while flying cross-country and never flew another plane. One of the aircraft of a group similar to the Flying Samaritans crashes in Baja California the following week, killing all aboard.

I agree to stop flying.

Pidge makes a delicious Thanksgiving dinner for all of us. Her home at Coastline, Malibu, is being sold. She and her husband-to-be are leaving the rat race and pressures of Los Angeles, to run a business in Mendocino, a beautiful county I had discovered years before moving to California.

"I don't blame you, Pidge," I say. "I was at The Heritage House once. The place is full of magical people, like the elves I imagine living in the enchanted redwood forests, which cover the mountains and fill the glens and run into the sea. But I will miss you."

Pidge can handle Richard better than anyone. He admits to me that at one time, he had been in love with her.

I mention that men sometimes feel this way about their daughters. Fortunately, he has never acted on it.

"Why not discuss it with her and clear away the cobwebs?" I suggest.

He promises me that he will. I never hear anything more. He skirts the issue like he did with Bob, his brother, and his need for financial help. Richard does not like vulnerability.

Thanksgiving is our last day of happiness. Our children join in. The next morning, after reviewing the X-rays Dan Amick had sent him, Dr. Matsumoto orders Richard to check into Cedars-Sinai Hospital.

Leslie Waldo, my colleague in psychology, is in my living room with me when the call comes from Richard now at the hospital.

"I have cancer, oat-cell, the worst kind. I have a month to live."

"I'll be right over," I respond coolly and hang up the phone.

"He has a month to live!" I repeat dully.

Leslie rescues me as I sob in his arms just as he has done once before. The first time I broke down was at the end of *One Flew Over the Cuckoo's Nest*, and I relived the electroshock at the mental hospital. Leslie had held me until the theater emptied.

This time I cut off the tears. "I have to get to Cedars as fast as I can," I said.

The bright colors of the wide, airy hallways belie the reason for Cedars-Sinai's existence. It does look like a hotel. I enter Richard's room and sit down on his bed. We say nothing. We wrap our arms around each other and cry. For how long I don't know. It is the last time we mourn together.

My denial system is as strong as Richard's. I refuse to believe he can die. I have studied with a medical doctor, Carl Simonton, an oncologist. Seventy-eight percent of his cases, all terminal, went into remission. Richard can go into remission too. Diet. Friends. I know Myrna Miller, a psychotherapist for cancer patients. She gives me a list of people to call. Two pages more of names of people who have gone into remission. Pidge and I read everything. We decide the real enemy is chemotherapy. Richard must not have chemotherapy. But we cannot guard him day and night. When we are not there, they give it to him. Richard does not realize what he is signing. His fans call with more advice.

I know of places to go for treatment in Europe and Mexico, but he will not budge from Los Angeles. He just sits in his bed at Cedars-Sinai. He is now bald, and looks like a movie mogul, barking orders, making demands, allowing no one in his room except one male, Irish nurse and the doctors. Everyone else is incompetent. Cedars-Sinai tolerates it all, accedes to his wishes in everything—but the chemotherapy.

Dr. Matsumoto apologizes. While testing Richard in July he had forgotten to do the back probe. I want to sue, but Richard will not hear of it. Later, much later, after my anger diminishes, I too thank Dr. Matsumoto for forgetting. But not now. I smash my hand through a wall. Ten years of therapy has taught me to unleash my feelings. I do. I pound the walls and scream at God to save Richard.

A publicity agent I know volunteers to help with the press. *The National Enquirer* runs upbeat stories about Richard's battle with the Big C. God cannot take him away so fast. I have just found him. He is on the rise. Requests for concerts are pouring in from all over the USA and Europe.

His agent, is beside himself, screaming at me over the phone, "Chemotherapy is what he needs!"

"Leave him alone!" I scream back.

When Richard begins attacking me too, I give up. I give him his Christmas presents and leave. Somehow, in less than twenty four hours, my travel agent has me on a plane to Mexico. I need my roots. I need the place I love, like he needs Los Angeles. There, among my friends, I can find myself and my strength.

I am gradually going out of my mind.

Chapter 21

Before I leave I go to see Pidge. I try to tell her (albeit incoherently) why I am leaving. She suggests I see her therapist. I only want her to know that Richard will be alone and ask that she check in on him while I am gone.

How incongruous everything seems in Mexico. Richard calls every day. I take the calls in my husband's library where a portrait of Philip the Second of Spain's stern countenance reminds me of the adultery I am committing. Yet, I do not feel that I am an adulteress. I only feel guilty about the deception, not about the relationship between Richard and me.

My husband, Jorge, and I actually admit our infidelities to each other in an uncharacteristic moment of intimacy. In some strange way, this is progress for us. At least it is better than when he terrorized me by pointing guns at my head threatening my life, accusing me of things of which I was totally innocent. I had felt guilty then, too, and yet I had done nothing. Like a child I wished him dead, not knowing how else to fight back. I dreamed he was killed in an automobile crash. Fifteen major accidents had not made an indentation in him.

How much my husband resembles Philip II! Like father like son, I observe.

Richard calls. "I miss you. Come back, I love you."

Is he talking to me or to Rita? More and more I am doubting his love for me. More and more I obsess on that question. It haunts my every thought and action.

What the hell difference does it make? I ask myself. *He's dying.*

But I can't deal with his dying, so I continue obsessing. I still take the calls in my husband's library. I prefer to have him present and listening to me, than for him to listen in from elsewhere. In that eighteen-room house, listening in is easy to do.

The rounds of parties begin. My daughter, Alexandra, accompanies me. The Cueto's Christmas Eve, the Benjamin's, they are all old friends with whom I can feel safe. Being with the de la Vega's, even being with my brother-in-law, somehow seems safer than going back to Los Angeles.

My daughter looks much too thin and complains of a valve problem in her stomach. I think she should see a specialist in the United States.

"Won't you come back home?" This is Richard's latest request, one of so many.

"I'll return for New Year's Eve," I reply.

"Tom Cooper wants us to go over to his house for New Year's Eve, if that's all right with you."

Alexandra offers to accompany me home, which is now Los Angeles.

Back in L.A. that morning the phone rings.

"Do bring Dick if you possibly can," Tom urges. "See if you can persuade him. Dick told me he can't come without his hair. I told him, 'Get a new rug.' Then he says the weirdest thing, 'I mean all my hair, Tom!' What's he talking about?"

"He's had chemotherapy," I explain. "He's lost all the hair on his body, his manhood, I suppose."

"Well, I've invited everyone. The party is really for him. Do whatever you can."

I promise I will. I know Richard does not feel like going. He is not strong enough. A month to live. The month is up.

Sometimes people get very weak before they get better.

We have weathered so many difficulties: financial problems, children, wives, my inadequacies, his alcohol. We have won.

We have survived them all. We love each other. With God's help we can win this one. I begin to wonder how I can reach God.

I take Richard to a colleague who has also trained with Carl Simonton. She has helped many cancer patients with Simonton's art therapy and visualization techniques. There is also a medical doctor Pidge found who has helped many people through a special diet. God will save him. Why would God have brought us together, just to take him away?

By evening Richard seems all right. Occasionally he coughs. We call the Cueto's to wish everyone in Mexico a Happy New Year. Because of the time difference, their party is already going strong. Before midnight we arrive at Tom's. It is such a kindness, such a thoughtful gesture. Everyone has come to say hello, wish us well and (say?) goodbye. The goodbye I am not willing to say, or even admit.

Vivian Blaine puts her arms around me and I try to hold back the tears. I do not want Richard to see me cry. He hates it if I cry.

"Get out of here if you're going to cry!" he always yells at me.

Without any words, Vivian understands and holds me. She loves him, too. In fact, well after midnight and too much champagne, Vivian grabs Richard's hand, "Shut up everyone. I want you all to meet the only man I loved who I never went to bed with."

Richard looks embarrassed, but pleased.

Dr. Kubler Ross is another person I think of calling. I attended one of her lectures a year previously, one on "Death and Dying." She helps the loved ones talk to the dying person, to say everything they need to say before it is too late. But then Richard is not going to die, so why talk about it?

Alexandra stays with Debbie at my apartment. During the day Alex acts as Richard's secretary while I am seeing patients. His fan mail has been mounting after the article in *The Enquirer*. He is meticulous about answering fan mail.

Thank God Alex is there.

Richard's doctors order him to send his son, Sean, back to his mother, Wendy.

Sean was sent home during the last siege in the hospital.

"I don't care if you are dying, you will have to take the children," Wendy tells Richard when she phones him at the hospital.

Wendy's denial is similar to my own. But at the time, how I hate her. She is threatening Richard's life. At least it seems that way to me when she unceremoniously dumps Sean and his belongings on a street near the Oakwood Apartments after Richard returns home. Sean knocks at our door wondering if he can come in. My hatred even extends to Sean, whom I dearly love. I, who have always put children first.

"Sean is a young boy and is in shock now that he knows his father is dying," Richard's attorney gently explains to me. "He needs to be with Richard."

We move to a larger apartment so that Sean will have space and Richard, too. I have a bed stand and a corner of a closet. It is a long way from the large home on the corner of Monte Libano and Monte Caucaso, surrounded on two sides by jacaranda trees in the Lomas of Mexico City.

I am gradually giving up my sanity.

Richard continues in the same agreeable manner he has been in since New Year's Eve. He obliges Pidge by seeing the nutritionist and me by seeing a psychologist. He sees his oncologist also.

Blake Edwards encourages Richard to rewrite *Reprise*. We discuss the television special I had named *America Sings With Dick Haymes*. We listen to the tape Richard has made. He chose his favorite singers. He paced it well. He speaks of an album that he could make with Klaus Ogerman—Latin rhythms, a Bosa Nova background—always the best. We also speak of a religious album he wants to do, a Christmas album that will reflect the spiritual side he has felt all of his life and has never expressed except for a few recordings long ago of "Ave Maria" and "The First Noel."

The PR agent visits us in the Marina. He lends us his Gospel of Saint Thomas. The three of us sit transfixed listening to "As Time Goes By." The agent watches us as we hold each other's hands. No words. Misty-eyed.

"What's God?" Richard asks me suddenly, when we are alone. Before I can think of one of my trite answers, the building shakes, an earthquake.

"That's God," I say.

I check the newspapers the next day. No notice of an earthquake.

Chapter 22

Sean and one of Richard's friends help pack up and move our things to the new apartment across the way and up two flights of stairs. I am not pleased about the stairs. We need the space but...

I stand around not knowing how to help, paralyzed by something else. Richard's agreeable mood vanishes. I can do nothing right. In front of him I feel useless and in the way. I leave. I go back to my apartment fifteen minutes away. What is to become of me? The same thoughts his son, Sean, must be having. Sean has asked me if I would take him.

"I can't Sean, I have no way to take care of you," I answer foolishly.

Sometimes honesty gets in the way of common sense. As I drive back to my place I don't think I will ever go back.

"The greatest love is shown when a person lays down his life for his friends." These words from Chapter 15 of Saint John begin to tumble in my ears. The Vineyard, the ripe fruit He comes to gather. Is this what it means to put aside my aching heart and leave my door ajar?

By nightfall I find some peace somehow. I go back. I do not use my keys. I knock. Richard opens the door. He looks at me as if he is seeing a ghost.

"Sean said from the look on your face when you left, that you would never come back."

"What does Sean know? He's only thirteen."

Richard's patience lasts until the following Sunday when his coughing takes a turn for the worse. I fear pneumonia. By 7:00 PM, we check back into Hotel Cedars-Sinai.

Five lung specialists are called in from all over the city. They operate right there in his room while asking a myriad of questions. When Richard balks, I fill in. Their teamwork, their assurance, their energy, give me a respite. I feel what I have never felt with the oncologists—safe. My fear and hatred of doctors flees. I admire their skill, their swiftness, their logic.

By 1:00 PM they have finished draining the fluid from his lungs and pack in penicillin to stave off infection. They want to know where they can reach me during the night. I know what they mean.

Oh, God, no! Please. It's too soon. I'm not ready, I pray silently.

I wish I knew the names of those men who gave Richard that extra time to be with me. I would thank them. I go back to my place knowing he is in good hands. The call never comes. I am back at the hospital the next day.

Richard is sitting up, brightly and cheerfully chasing everyone out of his room. The movie mogul is back.

"Dr. Matsumoto is allowing me wine with every meal, so you can get me some beer at the deli. It's two blocks south of the hospital. You can't miss it."

I find myself sneaking his favorite beer into the hospital. I, who believe that his way to wellness is through prayer and diet, am doing exactly what I believe to be wrong. But then that seems to be my way of life, doing the opposite of what I believe is right.

"You will stay with me, won't you?" he asks me in a quieter moment. "When I leave here?"

I promise.

Dick Quine, his oldest friend, who at one time was married to Fran Jeffries before Richard married her, comes over. I mistakenly think they would rather be alone, so I excuse myself and join some friends who are having a party at the Beverly Hills Hotel. I think that I should do something besides see patients and visit Cedars-Sinai.

The press comes to the hospital. Our PR agent takes care of everyone. They do not need me, so I try to become inconspicuous in a far off corner.

"Are you ready to die, Mr. Haymes?" the reporters ask rhetorically.

"I've had everything, I know everyone, I've done everything," the inimitable Mr. Haymes replies. "There's only one thing I never had, love. And I have that now, too. Yes, I'm ready to go."

Friends of Richard's appear offering financial aid. Richard, after repaying me everything, asks me for three thousand dollars. I give it to him. Anything to make him feel secure. Anything, more if he wants it. I offer to send

Sean to school, but Richard would not allow me to. He will not take anything from me unless he is desperate, and then only what he absolutely needs.

"Hey, Richie," Lee Guber, the producer of *The Big Broadcast,* telephones. "You'll do anything to get out of playing Boston!"

I hate Lee Guber because of Detroit, but I have to laugh, anyway. Perhaps it is true. And the rollicking, up-beat calls flow in from all over the world.

"Everyone's called but Frank," Richard says.

"Well, what do you expect," I answer, "after you told him he had skinny legs when you saw him last in Palm Springs!" But I know Richard is hurt so I try to reach Frank Sinatra.

Milton Berle is the kindest of all. He does his best to put me through to Frank. I am on the line to Frank's suite in Las Vegas.

"Wait a minute," someone answers.

I wait and wait. Then try the number again. I can't get through a second time.

Dr. William Kroger, who has trained me in hypnosis, suggests some attorneys who can go to the record companies on contingency. Richard figures there will be at least two hundred fifty thousand dollars owed to him. Dr. Kroger sets my mind at rest temporarily. He knew Rita Hayworth and Joanne Dru.

"You couldn't possibly remind Richard of Rita," Dr. Kroger assures me. "You aren't at all like her. She was glamorous, not beautiful. If anyone, you are like his first wife, Joanne Dru. You both have that same natural beauty, the fresh outdoors look."

Roger, a family friend, is sitting next to Richard's bed. He offers to take Sean. I think that as a young man, very presentable, self-made and prosperous, Sean would be happy with him. Sean does not agree.

Suddenly Roger changes the subject from Sean. "Mr. Haymes, could I ask you a personal question?"

"Sure, why not?"

"To what do you attribute your incredible success with women?"

"How the hell would I know? Ask her." Richard points at me. "She's one of them."

I look at him, outraged. Something inside me clicks off. I walk out of his room without a word, intending never to go back. I calmly go home. Everything is over. No more listening to ex-wives by the hour. No more.

"I'm the one he really loved," the ex-wives would repeat.

No more of this nonsense.

I do not belong here. I am not part of this, I determine to myself. No more.

At home the phone rings.

Richard yells in my ear. "Come back here or—!"

I slam the receiver down. He calls back, still yelling.

I slam the receiver down again. The phone rings again. I pick it up.

"Dianne, I love you." His voice has changed. "I want to marry you."

I go back again, knowing this is where he and Rita left off.

Chapter 23

Richard and Joanne Dru are able to spend some time together, alone. I am glad. He never wanted to divorce her. She wanted to divorce him. I hoped whatever painful memories caused the divorce, they could be healed. If Richard could feel less guilty...

"How do I look," Richard asks one morning.

"You look fine, darling."

"That's because you love me."

Richard sends me out to buy fluffy pillows at the May Company for his homecoming. Before I leave, I overhear him on the telephone with his friend, Dick Quine.

"I don't know where the hell she is."

Meaning me, of course. I resign myself. I'm staying and can only expect the worst.

The therapist sees him once. He refuses to listen to her healing tapes. I go to see her.

"It's just as well he dies," she says. "If he lived and became famous again, he'd go off with another woman."

Amazing how people can say the wrong thing at the right time. This is not what I need to hear.

I quietly despise her for her incompetence. I go to another clinic to see specialists helping the families of the dying. This therapist wants to know about my childhood! I get up and walk out.

It is going to be just God and me. A Mormon minister comes. He performs the final rites conditionally, anointing Richard with oil. His words are a priceless relief to Richard and me.

Pat Boone sends a beautiful plant and a book. I try to reach him. He is a Christian; he might know about healing. I can't get through. Richard is very appreciative of Pat's thoughtfulness and doesn't expect him in person.

Richard's last request of me before Cedars-Sinai dismisses him, is to take him to his favorite restaurants: Scandia and the Polo Lounge.

At Scandia's my resignation is temporarily broken when Richard pushes me to the brink again.

"When I get back home," he begins, "you know how it is, I need more than one..."

I am instantly thrown back to that moment in November, when we returned from Detroit...

"I met a woman over at Casa Escobar today. Guess what?" Richard grilled me one evening. "She wants me to go over to her apartment with her and make love."

"So? A lot of men ask me to do the same!" I was angry.

Even then, knowing how ill he is (or do I? I never really allow myself to know how ill he is), I can't handle the pain of losing him. He is so desperately needing reassurance. But I can't give it to him. Not when it comes to other women.

"I met—" He does not have a chance to finish the sentence before my voice rises to a high pitch as I say, "No way." Heads at The Scandia turn in our direction.

"You always have to make a scene!" he replies.

Testing...one, two three.

He will die testing me.

By Valentine's Day, we are back at the Oakwood Apartments. He is sleeping soundly that morning, so I leave Valentine cards and presents on the coffee table where he will breakfast.

He greets me when I come home that night. "Coward, why didn't you give me the presents in person?"

I can say nothing. I wanted to give them to him in person. I called him. He had always called me every day to tell me he loved me. I thought his words were Hollywood jargon. I no longer believed he loved me. But I did want to tell him what the past year had meant to me. What he had done for me. I wanted to say...

"Richie, you gave me so much. There were moments when you cared. You looked after me. You knew me. You knew what I thought and felt before I did. You opened a new world to me where people said and did what they felt as they were feeling it. You showed me a kind of honesty I didn't know because I was always so busy being polite, putting myself down. Somehow, Richie..."

I never said those words to him. I would have cried.

At about 1 a.m. he wakes me. He needs to talk.

"I'm listening," I mumble as I keep falling back asleep.

"You're not listening!" he yells as he nudges me.

"Richie, I'm doing the best I can. I have to work tomorrow. I need to sleep. If I can't sleep here, I'll go home."

With that, I get up, go to the closet and proceed to dress. I feel a yank and sharp pain in the back of my head as he hauls me back to the bed by my hair like some wild animal. I break loose and slug him as hard as I can.

We both sit there, starring at each other, stunned. I leave.

Somehow, Richard, through you, I am healing the wounds my husband and Jose Maria have caused. Our relationship reopened the wounds. But this time I fight back and come back.

When I return a middle-aged man named Jones has arrived to take my place, someone Richard has met in a bar.

"Would you please not spend the night anymore," he tells me, eyes lowered. "Sean does not like you here at night. Jones will help me if I need anything."

My mind blanks. I feel savagely hit in the stomach.

Whether Sean has requested this, I never know. I do not ask. Perhaps Richard is embarrassed by the loss of his sexuality and body hair. Our lovemaking has become mechanical.

I agree sadly to the arrangement. I would come over at

seven or eight in the evening, stay until eleven or twelve when he is ready to fall asleep. Sean disappears into his room, and Jones vanishes, but not fast enough. What has been ours is lost. Although I have paid the rent, it is no longer my place. I have already been displaced. The candles are no longer burning in our bedroom, nor are they burning for me in the living room when I come in. We sit together and wait. Sometimes he will light the candles when the others are gone. He will take my hand and hold it until he is ready for bed. Then I leave.

I remember it is a Friday night, March 21, 1980, at 3:00 a.m. when his last call comes. I am wide awake, reading my *Bible,* the Saint James version my mother gave me when I was ten.

"What are you doing?" His voice is filled with bitterness and suspicion. "Have you thrown in the towel?"

"I don't know what you mean." I sit in the bed holding the *Bible.*

"You know what I mean."

I want to run to him, hold him, love him. Instead I ignore my intuition, get up the next day for traffic school to pay for the multitude of parking and speeding tickets. I do not stop by to see him on the way to LAX after traffic school, and instead fly off to spend the weekend with a friend in San Diego. I call Richard from the airport.

"I'm fine," he responds. "Have a good time."

I had met Bruce Creighton at a tennis weekend in Palm Springs. I visit him or other friends to take respites from the agony I am ignoring. The agony I will not allow myself to feel.

I wait for Bruce to dress for dinner when all of a sudden over the radio Richard's voice is singing:

"I love the East, the West,
The South, the North of you..."

After dinner, Bruce and I go dancing at a charming spot overlooking La Jolla. Bruce is a friend of the band leader.

"What would you like us to play?" the band leader asks me as he chats at our table.

I had been watching enviously some of the couples dancing, obviously married for long periods of time, and obviously in love. *How lucky they are*, I think, as I reply to the band leader to play whatever he wants to choose for me.

"This next piece is being played for Dr. Dianne de la Vega," he announces over the microphone. The melody of "I Love the East, the West, the South, the North of You" pours out across the starlit night.

I get the message and take a plane back to Los Angeles and the Marina.

"Dad's back at Cedars-Sinai!" Sean yells at me. "Jones took him."

I race there as fast as I can.

"In Memory of Love"

Chapter 24

I grab Alice, a puppet monkey that fits over my hand and arm. I had learned to amuse and educate children and old folks with puppets in Mexico City for one of our Junior League projects. I once entertained the traffic school class out of total boredom by taking Alice.

Now, as I hurry down the hallways of Cedars-Sinai, the nurses and doctors stop me to say, "Hi," to Alice. She looks alive. Even Dr. Matsumoto laughs.

"I'm afraid Alice won't help," he adds soberly. "He's on morphine."

What he meant, which I still refuse to grasp, is the pain is so intense that...that what?

In Richard's room, I lay Alice down, then put my picture on the bed, and remove the picture of Fran Jeffries.

I remember how upset I had been last November when Fran's picture had appeared next to mine in our bedroom.

"Richard, no way can I make love to you with that Greek sex-pot staring at us."

"Can't I have a picture of my ex-wife in my own apartment? She's an older friend than you are." The knife was in.

"Not in the bedroom."

She was removed to the living room near my daughter, Alex's, picture.

Now I am too numb to feel the knife wounds anymore. I want my picture next to him, and there it will stay. But it doesn't. Somebody is moving it, because Richard did not have the strength. Every day when I come, my photo is tucked in a drawer somewhere.

I sit by his side. He knows I'm there. He takes my hand. His hand feels weak.

"You know I'm an alcoholic," he says.

"Yes, darling, I do."

"You need to clear up your relationship with your husband."

I am surprised and say nothing.

"You know the sailboat I wanted to buy?"

"Yes, I do."

"I wanted to sail it to Hawaii," he continues, "in hopes that it would sink on the way in a storm."

"I suspected that was what you wanted. I would not have gone with you without a captain."

He drifts off again.

"Oh, my God," I pray. "Don't let him die."

Anna Poole, head of his fan club, and I synchronize our watches. At 7:00 PM, Pacific Standard Time, Wednesday, March 26, 1980, we have arranged for everyone who loved

Richard across the nation to pray for him. Anna's entire membership has been alerted to pray together.

Tom Cooper, Sara, one of my patients, her boyfriend, and I are at his bedside. I explain to Richard what we have planned. He seems pleased. Sara's friend places us around Richard. I am behind his head. He can't see me. Tom is at his feet. Sara and her friend are in the center, opposite each other.

"Where's Dianne?" Richard says suddenly.

"Jesus," I answer, "I'm here."

Whatever made me say Jesus, I wonder, instead of Richie?

From what source within me came that voice, I don't know. I seldom use His name (except in vain, on the freeways).

Our prayer begins as scheduled at 7:00 PM. We place our hands on him. He seems to fade in and out, though he thanks everyone for coming when we leave.

The next night is Thursday.

"I love you, and drive carefully."

I don't know those will be the last words he speaks to me alive.

I make arrangements for Ken, the minister of The Vineyard, Tom Cooper and Sara to join me Friday for another prayer session in Richard's room.

When we arrive on Friday, his door is ominously closed. A sign is on the door: NO ONE MAY ENTER.

I open the door. Or do I? It opens by itself. I see a nurse and a young man with brown wavy hair dressed in a green hospital gown, waiting for me. He raises his hand and beckons me in. I am pushed back by a nurse.

Ken pulls out his credentials and says, "I am family."

The nurse lets me in. Sara and Ken follow. Richard is lying immobile on the bed. I scream and faint on the floor. When I revive, I see Richard standing among the nurses, the same young man who beckoned me in. He appears as he does in his movie, *State Fair*, with brown wavy hair. The silver hair is gone. He is watching me.

I must be hallucinating, I think.

"Why have they given Richard's room to this young man, when Richard's body is still on the bed?" I hear Sara say.

Sara must have seen him too, I muse, not quite daring to believe. Ken and Sara take me downstairs to the lobby. Then Sara actually says what I thought I heard her say upstairs, "Who was that young man in Richard's room?"

"That young man must be Richard," I answer.

He died at 5:00 PM. It is now 7:00 PM. The nurses seem paralyzed.

Tom Cooper is waiting for us in the lobby. We put our arms around each other and cry. Ken takes me home for dinner. Ken's wife speaks to me of death and of life. Her words are soothing and true, like the Mormon minister's had been. I wish I could remember what they both said.

My daughter, Connie, is arriving at LAX from San Francisco. Ken wants to take me but I insist on going by myself. I need to be alone.

The next morning, I open my front door onto the terrace. The sun is shining brightly on my rose bushes. I am still mercifully in a daze. At my feet on the doorstep, I pick up one single red rose, wrapped in baby's breath.

The enclosed card reads, "In Memory of Love."

I know Richard sent it. I do not know how. I just know he sent it. He is the only one who knew that I used to bring him roses from my garden.

He would say, "I should be bringing them to you."

Part Two

Anything Goes

Chapter 25

Someone is driving me (it must be my sister, Carol) to her friend's home in Topanga Canyon. All afternoon, I lie down in the tall grass, far from her house, not close to her flowers. Even the vibration of the flowers is too strong.

Oh, God, why, why, why?

The next morning, eyes closed, I see Richard for the second time since his death, seated in an old bi-plane. He is dressed like an aviator from the Lafayette Squadron, vintage helmet and goggles. *How bizarre*, I think. *He hasn't flown in years, not since he blacked out at 10,000 feet, a long time ago.* As he descends from the old-fashioned bi-plane, on the side I read Spirit of '76.

Years will go by before I fully understand what that means.

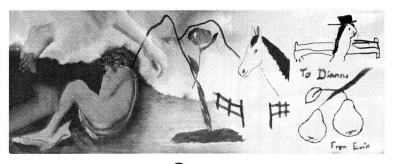

Chapter 26

The agony of his death continues. Mornings: I lie down on the floor and allow my body the freedom to writhe in pain for twenty minutes, my self-indulgent, daily meditation. Waves of anguish sweep through me, smashing me onto a bitter beach, broken into a thousand shards. I struggle through until bedtime and merciful sleep.

We are all bits and pieces of each other, broken off, floating in space, hoping to connect to some whole again.

Shari picks up one of my pieces. "Dianne, Peter and I want you to come to Kihei, stay with us. A group of people are gathering to prepare for next year's OneEarth Conference in Hawaii. Do join us."

I agree.

Sunny Lash calls the day before my departure. "Richard is here. He's telling me to tell you to visit Charles Lindbergh's grave in Maui."

Humoring her I ask, "Where is it?"

"It's near a church, an old colonial church. I just saw it on TV. They were doing a story on Anne Morrow Lindbergh. I didn't turn on the TV, it was simply on when

I walked in, on a station I never watch Sunday evening and I know the TV was off when I left. Promise me you'll go."

"Thanks, I promise," thinking, *more nonsense*, but she is so insistent. Then I remember Richard's appearance as an aviator, the day after his death, in garb similar to the garments Charles Lindbergh wore in his photographs with The Spirit of St. Louis, May 21, 1927, in Paris.

None of this is real. I put it out of my mind. I have no frame of reference for seeing and speaking with the Dead. Betty Grable, Duke Wayne, my father, all waking dreams, vivid imagination.

My plane lands on Big Island. At the Hilo airport, I deplane to buy a gift for Peter and Shari. I choose a box of marmalade and jams because it looks English and is attractively packaged with an artificial purple orchid on top.

They greet me at Kahului Airport on Maui, placing a lei of purple orchids around my neck. I chose correctly. The symbols match. I am where I am supposed to be.

The cooler air and the drizzle of rain at the base of Haleakala, where Peter has rented a hillside house, soothes me. My envelope of grief evaporates in the fog.

"The first meeting will be tonight," Shari explains. "One of the men has two small children. Their mother is away on a trip to the mainland. Would you mind watching them while we work?"

Before I can register my disappointment at not being included on the planning committee," she says. "Here are some paper and paints the children can play with. Take the big room downstairs. There's also a TV. We'll be working upstairs in the dining-room if you need anything."

Two beautiful children, David and Erin, beam up at me. David might be five, Erin, possibly eight. We silently come down the carpeted staircase. Through the sliding glass doors of the lower room we see the last gray light before dark over the moist meadow beyond, hardly a scene for voluptuous, tropical Maui, more like a Scottish heath.

The children, diligently, noiselessly, paint and draw, a short distance from me. Within twenty minutes, they stand in front of me, holding artwork papers with arms outstretched. "This is our gift to you, Dianne," they chorus.

The first picture is by Erin. Over the cleavage of two mountains, suspended in air, floats a single, red rose, bisecting the point where a waterfall cascades into a pool below. I am flooded with joy. Richard is here.

The next is a horse near a country gate, a thoroughbred horse, with a knowing eye. Erin names her third painting, "The Flower Shower Cloud," a shower of red roses falling on the same graceful, elegant horse. The last painting of Erin's is a branch from a tree with two very ripe pears waiting to be plucked.

David's drawings are in pencil. The first contains a bear, a flower with a happy face, and a bird, not one I recognize. In the second, sea otters swim near a pinnacle where a larger bird with a bald head rests. Among the otters is a man smiling, who appears to be dancing. The third picture painted with black strokes reveals a floppy, stuffed horse, with legs extended, a top hat, and a boutonniere in pencil, added as an after-thought. No other pencil marks are visible.

I stare in disbelief at the sparseness of line. The oriental simplicity, clarity, and preciseness, as if some ancient Chinese artist guided their small hands.

Reaching out to me, the two children sit down beside me, placing their arms around me, holding me until Shari calls two hours later, hours that are minutes. The love emanating from these two children I have known only once before, when the beautiful lady appeared in my living room.

Chapter 27

A narrow alcove under a stairwell serves as my bedroom. I have one window overlooking the misty meadow.

Shari enters the next morning. "There's someone here to see you. He asked for Peter, but I know he's here to see you. His name is Michael David."

I meet Michael David, not his real name, but his chosen spiritual name. He informs me solemnly, "I am on the Path."

I begin by asking him about his family, his childhood. His problem centers around his father. In anger he tells of his father's neglect and inability to express affection. He regresses easily. His rage pours out. He smashes the mats with his fists, until exhaustion breaks down his defenses. His lean, strong 35 year old body doubles over in sobs. He stops. A flash flood. His eyes clear. His speech is less tangential. I notice his extraordinary resemblance to Sean, Richard's youngest son who is fourteen.

"Do you know where this is?" I query illogically on an impulse, pointing to the first of Erin's paintings, the rose and the waterfall.

"That's the Queen's Pool," he answers without hesitation. "It's not far. Would you like to see it?"

I nod. I am aware that I have moved out of my mind and into my senses. "I suppose you know where Charles Lindbergh is buried."

"No, but I have friends who live next to Anne in Hana. They'll know for sure. I'll take you there."

I am awake in a dream. Nothing is real. I am following a trip-tic not of my making to the Holy Grail. I do not know where it will lead. I only know it has something to do with Richard. Therefore, I follow.

Michael David spends the night. He has a sleeping bag near mine. At some point in the night, he begins to make love to me. I do not object. My eyes stay closed. Half asleep, Richard is here. How strange. He is making love exactly as Richard did without any need to. Impotency is not one of Michael David's problems.

Two days later he re-appears with a vehicle resembling a jeep, only larger, more like a Land Rover. We head out for the foothills of Haleakala, through a Corot-like pastoral scene without the dab of sunlight interrupting the grayness. I shiver in the endless drizzle until the road stops. We clamber down from the jeep, hiking across muddy fields, climbing over fences guarding the farmland, until we reach a sloping hill over-looking a steep ravine. Cows graze lazily ignoring the rain. At the deepest end of the ravine, a dark pool, 25 feet in diameter, receives the falling water bisecting the mountain above, the Queen's Pool. Standing at the edge I hear Richard speak to me, for the first time since his death:

"I am a King. You are a Queen. Swim in the pool."

Too wet and cold to resist I follow instructions. The pool is not inviting. A muddy swirl of impenetrable water beckons me as I remove my damp clothes. I swim once around avoiding the falls and hurriedly step out. I imagine what creatures lurk in its murky depth. But not snakes. I have been advised no serpents exist in Hawaii. As I retrieve my clothes, I become aware I am standing between the legs of someone fifteen feet tall. His face and stature remind me of the natives of Mexico painted by Siqueiros or Diego Rivera, bronze-skinned muscular men with long dark hair framing rugged features.

I turn back toward the dark water. A woman of equal proportions stirs the water as if the pool is a pot of soup. Intent on her task she ignores my presence. Michael David sees nothing unusual. I remain silently curious. We retrace our path to the jeep, my clammy clothes clinging to my numb body.

Chapter 28

Following a circuitous route winding toward the East at lower and lower levels, we are transformed, transported from dank, wet highlands into a Technicolor movie of brilliant color, warm sun, soft breezes drying us off. Crossing more fields we arrive at the shack of Uncle Bill, a friend of Michael David, introduced as a friend of Alan Watts. I knew of Alan Watts, the famous philosopher author, from a passage read over the radio from one of his books. For years I have been trying to locate this passage. Unfortunately, Uncle Bill does not have Alan's books, only memories of his alcoholism.

"Alan would try to stop. We'd all help him, then someone would come along who reminded him of who he was. He'd start in all over again. It was hopeless."

Memories: "I don't want to be famous again," Richard murmured to me when offers began pouring in from all over the world. "But I need the money." He knew Fame well, a cruel companion, irresistible. He knew the high ride on the crest of the mountainous wave of adulation.

He also knew the end, the heart-rending, back-breaking trough below. He knew the fear Fame forges into a false image, separating you from you, leaving that "you" floundering on a beach of disintegration. No doubt, Alan knew this, too. Alcohol brought them both temporary relief from Fame's forge and misfortune.

Bounding across the marijuana fields, Uncle Bill's industry, we leave his shack and ramblings behind to look for food to carry with us to Haleakala and Hana.

The mangos and papayas vie with each other in a contest of brilliant orange. Crimson and yellow flowers in profusion lower the ends of branches. The tulipan africano majestic in size, with papery, red flowers erect, sprouting upward through emerald leaves, bursts into flame under the rising sun. Date palms and traveler's tree's fan-shaped leaves filter the sea breeze, sounding soft, rustling whispers in my ear. I can hear the rainbow; I can touch the music.

The Pa'io General Store provides us with bags of colorful fruit, island sausage, and Hawaiian bread. With our stores in tow we begin the ascent of the volcano. We pass ranches raising anthuriums, heliconias, and proteas, unreal flowers, like celebrities, imitations of their own reality.

Near the summit, we are stopped by a road crew. I am furious at the time lost with Uncle Bill and Alan Watt's addiction. A two to three hour wait, until the crew decides to end their workday. Vegetation is sparse at this altitude.

Only silverswords break the monotony of the barren landscape. Impenetrable clouds are below our feet, above our heads, and within me. I wallow in my anger, a relief from grief, giving me, like sex, a tow-hold on the earth. Michael David, in awe, patiently pays the price.

The crew finishes. My bottom, sore from two hours seated on a rocky ledge, finds comfort in the jeep as we crawl up the last thousand feet. Eerily parting fog reveals a space station on a moonscape. In the crater basin below miniature volcanoes poke their red roses out of the mammoth mother crater. We climb higher. Across the strait separating Maui and Big Island, thousands of feet below, snow-capped Mauna Loa and Mauna Kea salute us. To the east a full moon rises. To the west the sun is setting. Facing the twin sentinels, I stand with arms outstretched, a moonbeam in my left hand, a ray of sunlight in my right, forming a horizontal line. A current of union races through me as I grasp the light from the east and hang on to the sun rays in the west. Silently the sun slips through my fingers and the moon rises.

Improperly clothed, in need of shelter, we build a lava lair to break the numbing wind. Baby clouds creep in on the rusts and reds below us in the crater reflecting ghostly shadows from the moonlight above.

Too cold to spend the night, we desert our lair and slowly descend. The next morning we awake on a cliff looking over the Pacific, and once more, palm trees for companions. Flat fields of sugar cane, luminous pale green in the bright sunlight, remind me of the fields of Cuernavaca as they vanish behind the endless, curves, crags, and glens hundreds of feet over the not-so-peaceful Pacific, dashing, spraying, deepening and dredging the bays and inlets along what is an unbelievably pot-holed, unpaved road to Hana.

Pink and white impatiens, brightening the dark rain forests, snuggle at the base of vine-covered paperbark and eucalyptus trees, nestling among giant ferns. The hodge podge of jungle watches over the precise rows of papaya, avocado, guava trees on the few flat spaces of patchwork below. Ribbons of water-falls, plunging to their demise, bring sustenance to the mosses, taro vines, bamboo, elephant ears, ginger plants, breadfruit, bananas and koa trees. The Royal Poinciana as flamboyant as the red, orange tulipan juts out at my elbow. Jacaranda and bougainvillea covering cottages appear as we approach Hana and come to rest at the legendary Hasegawa store for more supplies. A sign welcomes us.

RENTED VEHICLES ARE NOT ALLOWED TO PROCEED FURTHER.

I decide the sign is irrelevant. Anyone who manages to arrive on the one-lane, rutty road to Hana to read it deserves to continue on, which we do, until we, in our rented jeep, spy the thatched roof, hexagonal bungalow of Michael David's artist friends. They design covers for popular record albums. They invite us for lunch. Michael David says, "No," which I regret.

They point to Anne's house next door. "Would you like to meet her?"

Michael David says, "We have no time," which I also regret. Time? All the time in the world. I, who am walking around in timelessness. They invite us to spend the night. Michael David declines again and I regret again. They are showing me a book I wish to explore full of symbols of biblical dimensions written in automatic hand-writing.

Michael David moves to leave. Yes, they are able to tell us where Charles Lindbergh is buried.

Back-tracking on the path we traveled, back toward Hana, we see a fence, a gate, and thorough-bred horses. Erin's second painting. Astonished, I see on the left the century old country church, Sunny described, shaded by an immense banyan tree. Winding through the infinite city of roots clustered in clumps around the central trunk of the tree, I walk directly into the cemetery and to Lindberg's grave. A marker with his name reveals the message, "If you take the wings of the morning and dwell in the uttermost parts of the sea..." I do not understand.

Michael David sits gazing out across the ocean on the cliff-edge beyond the graveyard, writing. He hands me the torn sheet from his notebook.

"Dear Soul Star, Diana, Thank you for bringing the light to the most intense and meaningful channeling in my life..."

I read with difficulty the two pages he has written and understand his need to be alone. I do not yet grasp the message on Charles Lindbergh's grave.

That night the sea calms, the jeep seems less hard, the moonlight slithers through the rock caves forming pathways across the surf. The beauty is intense.

We return to Kihei. I reluctantly leave the verdant world of peace and plants, my best friends since the age of two, when I met my willow tree, and the daffodils broke through the snow in my back yard in Rocky River, Ohio.

Back to people and good-byes. "My years on Maui have come to an end. I'll meet you in Santa Monica."

Michael David drives away, leaving me once more with Peter and Shari.

Peter asks me to regress him to no avail. His way is through his intuition, and there it will remain. Eileen, his wife, and Dorothy, his friend, can channel. A master of manifestation, he is the voice of his own truth through his actions. I learn from him.

He graciously shows me Lahaina, the port for whaling vessels and pirate ships, centuries before. I can see Captain Peter with a roving eye on shore with friendly females of Polynesian ancestry much to the chagrin and disapproving glances of long-gone missionaries.

The magic of Maui. I remember U.S. Anderson's account of his travels in Maui and how Richard tried to locate him. I remember, too, Richard and I, in ancient times, a kahuna—together, one person on Mu—a drop of water over the waterfall, not yet split.

People throng to Peter's house, some to prepare for the 1981 OneEarth Conference and others to rejoice in the new world, God-inspired and God-sustained where "the ancient shall be renewed and the new shall be sanctified," according to the Chief Rabbi of Jerusalem before his death.

Chapter 29

Returning home, opening my screen door, I find a note. "Please call me and come for tea."

This is the first invitation I have received from a neighbor in the three years I have lived on Alta's magnolia-lined street.

Elaine Friedrich, the widow of an Episcopalian minister, completes for me the message of Charles Lindbergh's grave.

At tea I begin to tell her about Richard's death.

"I know Mr. Haymes. He used to bring his children to our Sunday School. The oldest one, Pidge, was in my class."

Encouraged by the serendipity, I jump in full force, "Do you by chance know this phrase, 'If you take the wings of the morning and dwell in the uttermost parts of the sea...?"

"Why yes, that is one of the psalms, I can't remember the number, but I'll look it up for you."

Elaine called the next day. "It's Psalm 139."

"To the Chief Musician, a Psalm of David," I read.

Verse 1: "O, Lord, thou hast searched me and known me."

I skim to Verse 8: "If I ascend up into the heaven thou art there; if I make my bed in hell, behold thou art there."

Verse 9: "If I take the wings of the morning and dwell in the uttermost parts of the sea;"

Verse 10: "Even there shall thy hand lead me, and thy right hand shall hold me."

I grasp some of the message. I hear Richard singing, "You know the only one for me can only be you, my arms won't free you. My heart won't try."

Detroit, last September, so many eons ago.

Sara, returning from Findhorn, solves the mystery of the rose wrapped in baby's breath when I share Erin's pictures with her.

"*I* brought the rose. It's funny, after we left the hospital room where that young man had taken Richard's room while Richard was still lying on the bed, I went home. My roommate and I felt someone was in the house with us. All I was getting was, G*o to the store and buy some flowers*, so I did. I would have bought you a spring bouquet, but this presence said, 'No, buy one single red rose and write a card in memory of love.' So I did, and left it early on your doorstep because I was leaving that day for Findhorn in Scotland."

"Sara, it was Richard," I say. "I know you'll think I'm hallucinating from grief but—here, look at these pictures. Do you recognize any of them as the young man you saw in Richard's hospital room?"

"No, I don't."

"You have never seen any of his old movies? I mean when he was young."

"No, I've never seen him except in person looking rather frail."

"Will you go with me to see *State Fair*? Tom Cooper is playing it at the Tiffany."

"Sure, why not?"

That afternoon, at the end of the film, Sara is silent.

"What's wrong?"

"I'm shocked. I can't believe this. But the young man in Richard's room was definitely Dick Haymes."

A week later Sara joins me for a jog in the park at the foot of Alta, my place of solace where, sitting on the grass propped against a palm tree for strength, I scan the borderless blue of sky and sea, clear my brain, no longer alone. Richard is beside me.

"Do you see what I see, Sara?"

"Yes, I do. Richard's lounging there on the grass," she answers pointing to the spot where I am also seeing him. "He's twirling a piece of straw in his mouth, his blue hat is cocked on his head. He's wearing his checked sport coat and he's looking his age again like when I met him."

Psychic Sara, I had forgotten her prophecy a year before Richard and I met, "You'll fall in love with someone very famous."

"Oh God, Sara. That's exactly what I'm seeing. What is

he saying? I can't hear him. I'm too overwhelmed."

"He says he's fine, having a lot of fun with all his friends who have passed on. He was given a choice to remain there or be reborn. He chose to stay. He says he was weak at the time of his death so sometimes he has to go back to the Source to be re-energized."

"Yes, the morphine and the cancer. Go on."

"He'll always be with you, although sometimes he's with his kids and grandkids. You'll never want for anything."

"Erin's third painting, the Flower Shower Cloud," I remember aloud. "Tell him I love him and I'm feeling embarrassed and guilty about what happened with Michael David."

Sara laughs. In fact, she howls. "Richard's telling me to tell you, `Who do you think fixed you up?'"

I burst out in a regalia of much needed laughter, matching Sara's, gulping in the sea air with a sigh of relief.

And then he is gone.

Sara invites me to a party that night. I push myself to go. At her condo, everyone is playing a game involving large sums of money. Not a gambler, I feel out of it.

Rumors infiltrate the evening that a group from Beverly Hills is on a yacht playing for $50,000 a piece. This game at Sara's is minor league at only $5,000. Other than a few dollars at bridge games, I don't find losing money a joyful experience.

"Come on, Dianne, put your name down here. There's a new block opening up." This from Sara. I recoil.

"It's Saturday, The banks are closed. I don't have that much with me," I respond, trying to escape.

Another female voice joins in, "That's O.K. I'll put up the five for you. Pay me back on Monday."

I am about to say an emphatic, "No, thanks," when the sound of a toad interrupts me. "Brdp. Brdp. Brdp. Do it. Do it. Do it." Richard's famous toad imitation.

I sign my name and know I have lost my mind. The stranger gives me her address.

On Monday, I go to Crocker Bank at Wilshire and Westwood. They have no cash. They say, helpfully, that since I am such a valuable customer, they will try to find me some. The teller explains, "There's an unusual demand for cash in Southern California, but money will be arriving from the east coast any day now. Meanwhile we can arrange for you to withdraw cash at our Santa Monica branch. They have a little left."

With only $4,000, I find the lady's house, sheepishly promising to pay the rest later. That night I do not sleep.

How could I do such a dumb thing?

I return the next day to her home to make calls. This pleases her, but my friends, whom I contact, are furious. A huge bouquet of red roses arrives for the lady. Seeing the roses, I rally and am able to sleep.

By Wednesday, subtracting my original investment, I have gained $15,000! What a way to be repaid! The $3,000 trapped in Richard's checking account paid back five times over!

I give thanks and leave for Mexico.

Chapter 30

Carol Steinmetz and Jimmy Seifert, both friends of Javi, are going to be married. The Steinmetz children, neighbors in Lomas Chapultepec, grew up with mine. I need to see my patients and friends in Mexico City. I need their joyfulness, a joy that takes precedence over the exigencies of life.

Carol is beautiful in white satin carrying a single red rose. At the end of the reception when the bouquet is traditionally thrown, Carol hands the rose to her maid who insists on giving it to me.

After the wedding I go with a group of Quakers, whom I had met before at a leper colony outside of Mexico City, to help some American prisoners—girls arrested for the possession of marijuana, held without charge or trial for more than a year; some, several years. Their families, the American Embassy, and various lawyers have made no progress in freeing them, nor in bringing them to trial.

On the way to the prison we pray in the car, asking God to open the prison gates to let us in. I had visited before. The Quakers had never been refused.

The immense wooden doors we knock on make us seem insignificant, standing in supplication before this colonial fortress. Eventually a window slides open. An old retainer peeks through, looking us over carefully, then asks us what we want, knowing full well we are there to see the American prisoners. We have plenty of time to pray before he returns with the prison directress.

The heavy doors creak open permitting us entry. As they slam shut I feel a brief gasp of fear. Will they let us out? Nonsense, I know.

The girls welcome us. We are allowed to go to their living quarters.

On market days, twice a week, the prisoners purchase what they need to cook their meals on individual braziers, similar to those used by taco vendors on the street corners of Mexico City. Money needed for these purchases comes from home. Their decorated cells, except for the braziers, resemble any college dormitory. At the moment they are busy putting up their hair for a party tonight with the American boys ensconced in a near-by prison. The Mexican authorities escort the girls there and back, allowing them to spend the night if they wish. Some do.

In the group therapy session, I ask them, "How could you be so foolish not to heed the warnings from the State Department when you crossed the border?"

"Why should we believe the State Department. Look at Nixon."

I take their names and addresses to send to my daughter, Connie, in Geneva, Switzerland. She is working with people on the Human Rights Commission. Soon after, I read in the Los Angeles Times that the girls have been released. Did the message from Geneva to the Mexican government help? I will never know. I hope so. I feel relieved. Helping others relieves the pain I try to ignore.

Roses continue to rain, at weddings, at airports, wherever I happen to be. I fly to Alaska. My son, Javi's, fiancée, Belinda, greets me at the airport. "I meant to stop and buy you a red rose, but I was afraid I'd be late."

I have told no one except Elaine Friedrich about this phenomena of the red roses. No one has seen Erin's Flower Shower Cloud nor the red rose suspended over the waterfall, except Sara.

I travel to Mt. McKinley. The ranger guides us through the foothills, finally, stopping at a bird sanctuary, we see hundreds of birds exactly like the one David drew on Maui. I run through a field of blue forget-me-nots on a hillside, and, across a small lake I watch a mother bear and her cubs, sliding down a glacier, splashing into a pool. Mother bear swats and scolds the cubs for running off to play; the forget-me-nots and mother bear are also in David's drawings. I feel the freshness of the untouched Alaska in my veins.

I feel you near me, Richard.

No, I shall never forget you, nor your music, your ballads of love, the torment in your soul, your humor, your hidden days of despair, the days of wine and roses you helped Blake Edwards write. The words you wrote and the words in your songs were your affirmations. You believed in them. No,

I shall never forget. They are a part of me. They are the song in my heart.

In Valdez, I fish for salmon with Javi's friends. I, the novice, am the only one to catch salmon. My companions look exasperated as one salmon after another jumps off my hook. Finally a fifteen pounder catches hold, and before I can lose him, one of the experts leans over and snares my first salmon in a net. Packed in ice I send him back to Anchorage.

Doing a back-stroke all around us are otters, David's otters, sailing by with their babies on their tummies. I look up at the glacier cliffs surrounding the bay of Valdez. I see the horizontal turquoise streaks visible through the white translucent ice. In front of me, a flat-topped pinnacle, an off-shoot of a near-by mountain, holds David's bald eagle.

Need I see more? My eggshell cracks. My caterpillar legs glued to earth and pain crystallize into angel wings. I can fly. I can fly safely home.

The return flight from Alaska stops in Seattle. A man I do not know asks the stewardess for the seat next to me, although there are other empty seats. He shows me a book, *The Airmen Who Would Not Die*. "You must read this book," he says. "My name is David Rose. I'm a waiter in Los Angeles."

I think him odd. The symbols evade me. I ignore his message. A week later he calls. He must have found my number in the phone directory. "Have you read the book?"

"No!"

"Then I'll bring it over."

Two hours later, taking two buses from West Hollywood to Santa Monica, David Rose appears at my doorstep, book in hand—an authenticated account of a pilot who died in a crash over the Azores in 1928. His attempts to warn the British government of the impending disaster of their dirigible 8101 in 1929, were unsuccessful because, at first, although Christians, they refuse to believe in life after death. Like me, they refuse to believe that communication exists between the two dimensions.

The book in my hand is real. David Rose is real. The children on Maui are real. Only the superficial and ill-trained scientists who deny the anecdotal evidence are unreal. They are their own hallucinations as they proceed to deny the reality of the universes in which we live. The fragrance envelops my house and disappears. My neighbor, Henry, investigates but cannot find the source. I do not tell him. He will never believe me. Perhaps I do him a disservice.

Shari and Peter send two postcards. Both have the same picture of the demi-god, Maui, holding back the sun over Haleakala so that his mother will have time to dry the bark she makes into clothes. The picture on the postcards is identical to the fifteen foot man I saw at the Queen's Pool.

I search the pages of Jung's *Mysterium Coniunctionis*. My symbols are all there: the Sun, the Moon, the Branch, the Goddess, the King, the Queen, the Salmon, the Eagle,

The Toad. "Opposites either confronting one another in enmity or attracting one another in love."

The Union, the underlying principles of alchemy, "dissolve and coagulate," chaos followed by integration..."sun and moon are marriage partners who embrace on the twenty-eighth day of the month."

Richard died March 28, 1980. No more muscle-laden armor of scientific denial keeps us apart; only the veil of Maya, until my death.

Yogananda, the *Bhagavad-Gita*. I read his autobiography. I visit four of his centers. I reread the Gita. In the Upanishads, I find the twelve steps, the same words of St. Francis who gleaned them from Jesus, who found them in India, or drank them from the Living Water.

A group of Russians stands at the gates of the Lake Shrine on Sunset, begging to be allowed in after hours. They have no time left before they must return to their country. The monk opens the gate. They stand in awe of the monuments to each of the earth's five major religions, Christian, Buddhist, Jewish, Hindu, Moslem, "This would never be allowed in our country," they acknowledge.

In Lourdes, France, 1954, I kneel in the grotto before Bernadette's Lady of the Immaculate Conception, and pray for the restoration of my eyesight. I hate my glasses. "Please let me see," I plead. I do not realize what I have asked, for in the Lady's world seeing is knowing.

"Mary, Mary quite contrary"

Chapter 31

A booming voice awakes me in the middle of the night, the day before I depart for London and Findhorn.

"Your name is Mary and you are from Scotland."

I cease packing and race to the UCLA library. "I need a history on Mary, Queen of Scots," I ask the librarian not knowing anyone else by that name in Scotland. I am trembling so much I have to ask her to find the Stuarts' history for me. I xerox the part about Mary and her parents. I take it outside hoping food and sunshine will calm me enough to focus my eyes on the small print. I meet James V of Scotland and Mary of Guise, a French noble woman, as well as their tragic daughter, Mary.

For two hours waves of fear sweep through me in uncontrollable shaking as the words revive horrific memories in my body of betrayal, rape, murder, imprisonment, injustice, illness, poverty and finally crushing blows to the neck and head.

"I am a King, and you are a Queen" were Richard's words on Maui at the Queen's Pool. I had never taken them literally. However, my body does. The ax on my neck, the shame, the grief, the rage are all real.

From LAX to Heathrow, I attempt to concentrate on the workshop I will give for the 1980 OneEarth Conference, "The Miracle of Relationship." I am unable to focus.

Although she has not seen me since I am two, Pat Ellacott invites me to stay in London with her family. I tell her guardedly of my spontaneous past life experience. She does not flinch. On the contrary she recommends a better researched, recent publication.

My London tour takes me to the spot where Ann Boleyn lost her head by order of Henry the VIII. I walk by the graves of the literary giants in Westminster Abbey, remembering the two thousand lines of poetry I memorized in my junior year of high school.

I pass on the left side of the naive, glancing up at the stone casket above my head. "Elizabeth I, I continue around the naive, another stone casket. I tiptoe up to look on the serene stone face of Mary, buried, opposite her cousin, the two queens resting peacefully, side by side in death.

My body or soul take over. I release an overwhelming sob of grief and remorse. I accept my violent death. I no longer, as the proud Queen, have need to hold back the shrieks of anguish as I did in 1584. Fortunately, the Abbey is empty.

Pat drives me to Windsor Castle, escorts me through the chapel, shows me where "my progeny are buried." We arrive at a stone marker in the wall, "the Duke of Norfolk." Pat suddenly rebukes me, shaking her index finger in my face with unaccustomed fury, contorting her fine-chiseled features. "You are responsible for his death. Because of you he plotted to overthrow Elizabeth."

I see the hatred of a forsaken wife, widowed before her husband, the Duke of Norfolk, could divorce her, depose Queen Elizabeth, and marry the Mary of Scotland. The wily Elizabeth removed his head.

"Mary, Mary quite contrary. How does your garden grow?" I remember the sing-song game we played as children, chanting, "with silver bells and cockleshells and pretty, little maids all in a row."

I was only a pawn in a game.

Chapter 32

Entering the compartment on the train to Inverness, I am welcomed by April, a wholesome Australian mother of two enroute to the OneEarth Conference, only fitting that my invisible guides provide me with a proper companion for the last segment of my journey north to Inverness, Forres, and Findhorn. The abnormal is normal; the normal, bizarre.

Out of the shallows, shattered by the depth of life's soul, I am a trapeze artist on a long and painful flight to the light in the heart of me suspended in mid-air, afraid to let go of one bar until I catch another, arms outstretched, groping in the dark. I am sustained, I am led, I am guided, I am sheltered, I am fed, I am loved and I am healed. I cry out, "Take over whoever you are. I cannot run this show. I can not even write an outline for a conference I am giving tomorrow." I clutch to my chest like an ancient manuscript, the drawings from Maui.

April breaks my reverie holding Erin's painting of two ripe pears in tandem on a branch, "This is John 15," she reads. "Every branch in me that beareth not fruit he taketh away; and every branch that beareth fruit he purgeth it, that it may bring forth more fruit."

April's "Aussie" accent in "Old English" continues on with authority from her King James version of the Bible, authorized by James the First of England, né James the Sixth of Scotland. My son?

"Abide in me and I in you. As the branch cannot bear fruit of itself, except it abide in the vine; not more can ye, except ye abide in me."

The gray stone mansions of Forres are massive beside the delicate, colorful rose bushes guarding their entrance. October is neither cold nor dreary, not even misty in the bright sunlight. Leaving Forres, we pass the greenest of greens on Cluny Hill, a 19th century hotel, 180 years old. It is built more like a palace, commanding a view of the golf course and Forres, beyond. It is my home for the next ten days.

At the front desk, I receive the schedule of events for the conference, a room assignment and my work/play schedule for those of us remaining to experience the Findhorn Community founded through spiritual manifestation, unintentionally, by Peter Caddy, his wife, Eileen, and their friend, Dorothy McLean.

The unexpected luxury and elegance includes a white tiled bathroom of sitting-room proportions where rainbow colors splash the walls from sunlight refracted through stained glass windows. The only problem with the exquisite bathroom is its uniqueness; only one per floor.

"I'm Joan from New York," a young lady introduces herself as I lift my suitcase onto one of two twin beds.

"Dianne, from L.A." I glance at the pamphlet Joan is digesting. "Isn't that John Pierrakos' group?" I recognize the logo.

"Oh, you know him? I've studied with him for sometime."

"Me, too. He taught bioenergetics to our Gestalt Group in Mexico City." We hugged.

Claude Curling, a quantum physicist from King's College in London, opens the convocation with, "If you take the wings of the morning, the angel wings..." I gasp. Of course, the angel wings, the guardian angel wings. I say to myself and to Richard in step with Claude," and dwell in the uttermost parts of the sea, even there shall my heart, hold thee;"—a Freudian slip of love, "heart" for "hand," on angel wings.

Shari speaks next, openly describing her relationship with Peter. I squirm. Remnants of Rocky River, Ohio, pervade me. At Findhorn nothing is shoved under the proverbial carpet. Total vulnerability prevails. I am grateful Peter's wife Eileen has not yet arrived. In 1580 royalty were not yet airing intimacies.

My first conference, "Stress Factors of Cancer," begins that morning. I base the information on the training I received from Carl Simonton, M.D., whose techniques, including psychotherapy, sent 78% of his terminal cases into remission. I had begged Richard to see him. He adamantly refused.

A German physician refutes me vociferously. I do not retreat. "Cancer, like most illnesses, is caused by stress, leading to the collapse of the immune system. The 6,000 cancer cells we need to eliminate daily flourish."

Early in the afternoon, I go unprepared for my second conference, an album of Richard's music under my arm. Thirty people from around the world are waiting for me. I ask them to form a circle. Claude Curling sits directly opposite me; on my left a lady from Venice, next to her the German doctor. I am surprised. On my right are several people from the Findhorn Community. Others are from India, France, and even Scotland.

I begin, "Would everyone, please, introduce themselves and, if possible, let us know why you have come."

A woman from the Community raises her hand. "Although we are supposed to be so open here, I find I am having problems communicating with my husband." Others speak, but her words direct me.

"I would like to tell you about the miracle of my relationship with Dick Haymes, whom I will call Richard. He told me once he loved me because I was the only woman he ever knew who related to him, Richard, and not his image. He hated for me to use his stage name. Many of you are too young to know his music or his movies, so I will introduce him by playing the last song he ever sang in public. He sang it to me. At the time, I was sitting in the audience in front of him in Detroit, Michigan, the closing night of the musical *The Big Broadcast of 1944*. He sang the song written by his friend Harry Warren,

'The More I See You.'"

Boundaries fall away with his music. Illusions of separation vanish like the night he drew us all together at the Bonaventure, Doubleday party.

"Can you imagine, how much I love you," his warm baritone voice floods the room.

"The more I see you as years go by. You know the only one for me can only be you, my arms won't free you, my heart won't try."

I switch off the music. For the next hour I relive the joy and the pain of our relationship, the communication and the lack of it. Finally I say:

"The shock of his death wakes me up from a deep sleep. I am no longer able to deny who I am, who we all truly are the soul of God on earth. You see, each and every one of us is a Star like Richard was, who has volunteered to come down and help with the re-creation."

The prolonged silence following my last words startles me back to the conference room. Tears stream down the faces in the circle. The woman from Venice is kneeling at my feet, pressing a rock of amethyst crystals into my hand. I am puzzled, also, to see the German doctor weeping. Claude breaks the silence, "Dianne, you have zapped me twice. May I see you later this afternoon."

Late in the day Claude guides us with imagery into hidden rooms. Behind my secret door, I see a beautiful lady, her long brown hair softly floating as she barely touches the sphere under her feet in apparent weightlessness, like a painting of the ascension of Mary by Murillo.

Claude, continuing the guided imagery, asks us to leave the secret room and imagine a chair in which we will sit. I find myself sitting in a sturdy, high-backed wooden chair, much like a medieval throne. Richard is standing behind me. He is placing a crown upon my head. I feel the weight of it. He places a scepter in my left arm and an orb in my right hand.

Chapter 33

Ian, a Scotsman, offers to drive me to Edinburgh. He is one of the guests, like myself, at Findhorn, also one of my team of twelve, who have weeded gardens, cooked in the kitchen, and dusted the rooms of Cluny Hill.

He stops at Falkland Palace. "Here is where Mary lived when she was happy. In fact, she was born here. Her father rebuilt this palace for Mary's mother using French masons, to make her feel at home. That is why it has that Renaissance look. Her mother was a Guise from France. But he never recovered from the loss of his first wife whom he had loved so much and soon continued his philandering, populating the country with his illegitimate children. He died in this palace from wounds of war and shock upon hearing all of his legitimate sons had been killed in battle. The final stroke for him was to learn a daughter was born. He died the day of her birth."

I shuddered, remembering how my father wanted a boy so much at my birth that my older sister called me, "Jerry," for the first year of my life.

"Mary could ride out from here," Ian continued, jumping across the low walls and hedges to the fields beyond. Probably the only happiness she had were these brief visits to this palace, away from the court, the treacherous nobility and Knox's church.

"She was a good Queen, good to the ordinary people. On these rides into the countryside, she visited the people in their homes to ensure they were treated fairly and had enough to eat. They later regretted her overthrow. She was a worthy administrator. Her son James, was less interested in the people."

I wonder if everyone in Scotland knows as much as Ian about Mary, Queen of Scots. Ian leads me to the palace chapel. I kneel. The sun filters through the stained glass windows. I pray for Peter and Eileen. I feel they are my parents if I am Mary. The first time I met Peter, the same uncontrollable trembling happened, the same as the day I waited for Richard on our first date. I walked through a crowd of a thousand people at the Pasadena Convention Center and picked Peter out. I needed no introduction. We sat down and talked. If this is true that he was my father, it would be my first meeting with him. He died on the day I was born. Ian shows me the room where he died.

My mind wanders back. I look up at the windows in the chapel. I see Mary's coat of arms the fleur-de-lis in blue, like my own father's shield, the DeMarinis coat of arms, bestowed for deeds of valor or merit, a custom as ancient as the Jehovah tribes of Israel, secured by the humblest as well as the highest.

My arms are azure, the fleur-de-lis argent; the crest,

above the shield on a rock sable, a horse, passant, proper, Erin's horse, the thorough-bred horse behind the gate and again in the Flower Shower Cloud, come home at last.

Neither blue on silver nor silver on blue. I am not the shield.

I am the light passing through.

The End

The Living Waters

At Charles Lindbergh's Grave

You Shall Never Want for Anything

Dianne de la Vega

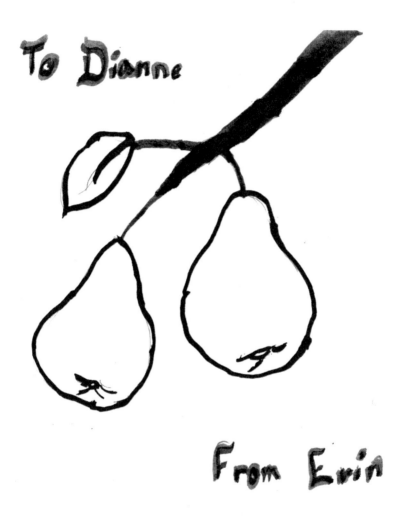

"Every Branch that Beareth Fruit" (John 15)

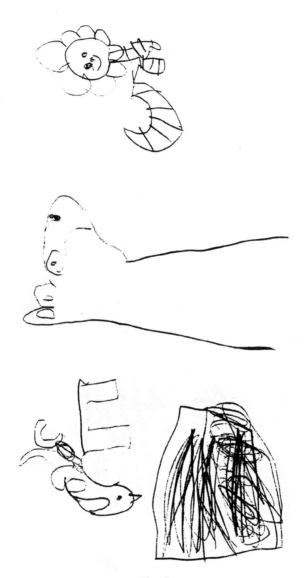

Alaska
The Bird, Bear and Forget-Me-Not

Valdez
The Otters, the Eagle, and Richard

The Boutonniere and Forget-Me-Not
Richard in Top Hat

Hawaii
The Demi-God Maui

De Marinis

My Father's Coat of Arms